Stay Out of Court!

The Small Business Guide to Preventing Disputes and Avoiding Lawsuit Hell

Andrew A. Caffey

Ep
Entrepreneur
Press

Managing editor: Jere L. Calmes
Cover design: Pay-Fan
Composition and production: Eliot House Productions

This publication is designed to provide accurate and authoritative information in regard to the subject matter covered. It is sold with the understanding that the publisher is not engaged in rendering legal, accounting, or other professional services. If legal advice or other expert assistance is required, the services of a competent professional person should be sought.

Library of Congress Cataloging-in-Publication Data is available

Caffey, Andrew A.
    Stay out of court!: the small business guide to preventing disputes and avoiding lawsuit hell/by Andrew A. Caffey.
      p.   cm.
    ISBN 1-932531-26-2
    1. Dispute resolution (Law)—United States. 2. Actions and defenses—United States. 3. Small business—Law and legislation—United States. I. Title.
    KF9084.C34 2005
    347.73'9—dc22   2004061987

Printed in Canada

11 10 09 08 07 06 05   10 9 8 7 6 5 4 3 2 1

Contents

PART V

The Mindset Key:
Establishing an Ethic of Accountability

PART VI

Making the Lawsuit Go Away

Preface

THE BREATHTAKING EXPENSE, THE UNFATHOMABLE EXPENDITURE OF TIME, THE bruising, table-pounding threats, the shocking invasion of unrelated confidential matters: no wonder businesspeople and professionals detest the way the American court system resolves disputes.

As a business attorney, author, arbitrator, and negotiator of more than 25 years, I have watched my clients learn the hard way that courthouse cases are protracted and expensive and an ultimately unsatisfying method of resolving disputes. In the hands of too many attorneys, the courtly traditions of litigation mask a vicious game of lawful extortion in the name of justice that is far removed from the principles of justice. Lawsuits bring out the worst in legal professionals, forcing bar associations across the land to adopt written standards of basic civility. The abuses of the American court system have come to represent a disturbing weakness in our society, a niggling but growing flaw in our national character.

A recent *Newsweek* magazine, with the sensational cover headline "Lawsuit Hell: How Fear of Litigation is Paralyzing Our Professions," described how the fear of lawsuits is changing the way services are provided in medicine, education, religion, and other fields. Many competent providers are driven out of vital professional specialties by the high cost of lawsuits. There are no easy answers, of course. The magazine considered several ideas for industry-specific tort reform in the future and briefly looked at the grid-locked politics of litigation reform.

What can individuals, professionals, and businesses do to reduce the risk of being taken to court, and if they find themselves there, how can they limit the damage? As it turns out, there is much that can be done, some of it counterintuitive. I have spent years keeping my business clients as far away from a court of law as possible.

Future tort reform is not the answer to the paralysis that businesses and professionals currently experience. I expect tort reform to continue to be nothing more than a running sideshow in presidential election years, a classic throwaway campaign issue. We certainly cannot count on tort reform to provide any answers to the problems caused by the explosion of lawsuits in the first decade of the 21st century.

The answer for individuals, professionals, and businesses lies in an aggressive and common sense application of the principles and tools described in this book that I have developed in representing my clients. They break down into three fundamental areas: court avoidance skills, dispute resolution tools, and the necessary mindset to avoid and resolve disputes. Master these skills and use these tools, and you will greatly increase the chances that you will *Stay Out of Court!*

—A. A. Caffey
Washington, DC

This book is dedicated to the "Big Two,"
Marcie and Jack Caffey,
with love and admiration.

PART I

Welcome to Lawsuit Hell

Torts are lawyers' happy hours
Like double gins and fizz;
Spelled backward tort is trot,
Straight to the bank, that is.
—ART BUCK

It is certainly not news to most business people and professionals that american business is under attack by a sue-for-profit industry that is way out of control. Our litigation fixation has been gnawing on the legs of businesses and professionals for a generation, draining profitability, driving up insurance rates, and changing the way business is conducted and how people relate to one another in the workplace.

Defensive business practices are often ineffective when it comes to discouraging a lawsuit from being filed. The only way to meet this foe is to jump out of the defensive foxhole and face it squarely on the field of battle.

You can win this hand-to-hand combat, but you will need to sharpen your skills, clean and oil your weapons, and adopt the right mindset. We will explore all three of these components in this book.

Before you jump up and charge, though, it is also vital that you understand exactly what you're up against.

Why Is It So Damn Hot in Here?

THE CIVIL LAWSUIT INDUSTRY IS COSTING INDIVIDUALS, PROFESSIONALS, AND businesses in the United States billions of dollars every year. The precise dimensions of these costs are not easy to nail down, but estimates suggest that $205 billion is spent on all aspects of our civil litigation industry, with about 50 percent of that amount going to items such as legal fees, the courts, and administrative costs.

The other costs the public incurs because of this burgeoning industry are incalculable. Everyone pays a price when obstetricians leave communities because they can no longer afford their malpractice insurance premiums, high school coaches hesitate to make team selections based on their best judgment for fear of legal retaliation, or doctors order unnecessary tests not for medical reasons but as a kind of crude insurance against a later claim that lack of professional thoroughness led to an incorrect diagnosis.

The sheer absurdity of so many lawsuits titillates the media, and the stories appear almost daily:

- The city of Greenwich, Connecticut, takes a tough one-two punch: A local resident is murdered by a deranged stalker, and his widow sues the community for not doing more to prevent the murder, winning a $4.5 million settlement. Then a local urologist collides with a drainage ditch while sledding in the snow. The city should have done something about the ditch, he argues in his lawsuit, and a jury awards him $6 million. Greenwich leaders, desperate to shield themselves from ravenous lawyers, announce they may have to ban sledding, ice-skating, and "other high risk activities."
- A hungry husband and wife in Utah are dining at an open buffet restaurant (appropriately named the "Chuck-a-Rama") and are told they are eating too much sliced roast beef and are asked to leave the restaurant. The couple announces plans to sue the restaurant for hundreds of thousands of dollars.
- In a case of national notoriety, a customer of a McDonald's restaurant is scalded by a spilled cup of coffee and hits the jury jackpot with an award in the millions.
- Two boys dive into the ocean off a pier in Santa Monica, are injured when they land in the shallow water, and sue the pier owner (and win!) for failure to post a sign warning of the danger.
- A student is caught cheating on a test; when he is disciplined, his parents sue school officials for damages.
- A youth baseball coach is sued when he refuses to put a player on an all-star squad.
- A high school PE teacher is sued for verbally abusing an overweight female student in his class, and the jury awards $1.47 million because the young woman claims the teacher's behavior caused her to develop an eating disorder.

- Televangelist Jim Bakker's "Praise the Lord" ministries settle a class action with nearly 165,000 defrauded Christians for $3.7 million after 16 years of litigation. The lawyers get $2.5 million, and each victim gets $6.54.

Perhaps the highest price Americans pay is the weakening of a judicial system that has been a pillar of our national pride since the founding of the nation. For every court decision that wanders far away from public common sense, for every case that awards millions of dollars to a plaintiff for seemingly insignificant, inconclusive, or unconnected damages, and for every case where an aggressive team of attorneys is seen to be fabricating a claim or a class of plaintiffs, the civil court system is devalued in the public's perception. In people's minds, the courts become irrational places where the wheel turns and some lucky contestant and his lawyers walk away with a king's ransom. The courtroom has become unpredictable and in many ways has lost its dignity.

Businesses and professionals take the brunt of punishment in this out-of-control civil litigation game. The fear of being sued has invaded every aspect of our people's lives. The media has reported on the impact of those feelings. For fear of an allegation of a misdiagnosis, physicians order up a battery of tests that are not medically necessary, and the costs of medical care increase. Doctors are leaving practices where malpractice insurance premiums have driven them out of business. This pattern is particularly noticable in states with a history of high jury awards. Ministers, teachers, and coaches always have to be aware of the potential problems of touching the children and adults in their care and must go out of their way never to be alone or behind closed doors with clients, students, patients, or church members lest they be sued and have no corroborating witness for their defense. In order to protect themselves from lawyers, affluent cities are restricting everyday high risk activities such as ice skating, sledding, playground games of tag or dodge ball, and even the continued use of traditional playground equipment.

This is a picture of a society in judicial distress, and it is a dismal picture indeed. Rather than simply hoping to avoid lawsuits, every business and professional needs to develop a strategy that will counter the insanity that has become our civil justice system and even the odds as much as possible.

This book suggests just such a plan of action.

Litigation: A Voracious Industry Made in America

The new millennium has seen the birth of a phenomenon in the legal profession: the billion dollar global law firm. In 2003, the five largest law firms in the world each grossed more than $1 billion in total billings. The largest of these is the London firm Clifford Chance, which has 3,700 lawyers (680 of them litigators) in 19 countries and in 2003 grossed $1.5 billion dollars. That's $1,500,000,000!

Although three of the top five of the world's largest firms are British, the deeper ranks of the lawsuit industry are dominated by Americans: 25 of the top 30 law firms in the world are headquartered in the United States.

There are approximately one million attorneys in this country, up from 100,000 at the beginning of the 20th century. Seventy percent of the world's attorneys are located in the United States, and an astonishing 94 percent of the world's lawsuits are filed here.

Without question, the *legalizing* of people's lives is an American phenomenon. It is ours to understand and ours to confront. The reasons for the current predicament run deep in the national character. It is nothing short of the confluence of a commitment to the rule of law, unblinking (some would say misplaced) confidence in the judgment of citizen jurors, the functioning of society's imperfect checks and balances, the counterbalancing of institutional size and wealth in America, and the exercise of the ultimate strength and power of the American individual.

This confluence has produced a growing imbalance. The last 30 or 40 years have delivered a stunning list of extremes: the rise of class actions, excessive jury awards, contingency fee lawyering, advertising to drum up legal claims, and the billion-dollar-a-year law firm. What started out as an essential—and essentially conservative—arm of government has turned into a rip-roaring, All-American, for-profit industry, and its aggressiveness is bringing parts of society to its knees.

Civil Litigation: An Oxymoron

There's nothing civil about today's civil litigation. The traditional image of learned professionals as officers of the court stepping before a wise and decisive judge to make dispassionate but insightful legal arguments is fading fast. The reality of litigation in the 21st century is quite a bit more freewheeling, and inescapably nasty.

Rather than handle a case with professional detachment, many litigation lawyers have lowered their behavior to rudeness and combativeness in order to gain an edge, to show resolve, and to demonstrate toughness. This approach spills over into the deposition room and the courtroom where attorneys not only show contempt for one another but also thinly veiled contempt for the courts. Judges and state bar associations have taken extraordinary measures to reestablish a level of civility between litigating lawyers. The American Bar Association and state bar associations have adopted new rules for the manners and respect lawyers are expected to show one another, as well as ways to express respect for the court and the judicial process. Courses on professionalism are now required not just for new members of the bar but for experienced attorneys as well.

Lawyers on either side of a case often adopt a scorched earth policy of contesting every possible detail of a case, and throwing every conceivable motion in front of the judge in order to run up and accelerate the cost of the defense.

The problem runs deeper than having too many lawyers streaming out of law school. Civility has disappeared in large part because plaintiff's lawyers are now directly interested parties in the outcome of their cases because of the increasing size of jury awards. Professional detachment has seen its day.

Jury Verdicts Find the Stratosphere

The size of jury awards has been spiraling higher. In 1999, the ten largest jury awards to individual plaintiffs totaled $9 billion—triple the amount of the top ten awards in the prior year. By 2000 these figures were small change: a smoker was awarded $1.2 billion (subsequently reduced to $100 million). And then came the all-time jackpot, a $246 billion settlement between the states and the tobacco industry. In her noteworthy book *The Case Against Lawyers*, (Broadway Books, 2002) Catherine Crier called this, "The largest redistribution of wealth to the smallest number of people in the history of the world. This payout does not refer to the monies awarded to the sick but the billions that went to a cluster of attorneys for their work on the cases."

There is some good news. In 2003, the U.S. Supreme Court for the first time offered a rule of thumb that applies to cases where punitive damages far exceed the amount of compensatory damages awarded, thus violating due process. In *State Farm Mutual Automobile Insurance Co. v. Campbell*, decided April 7, 2003, the court struck down as grossly excessive and arbitrary an award of punitive damages in the amount of $145 million with compensatory damages of $1 million—a ratio of 145:1. The Court said, "Few awards exceeding a single-digit ratio between punitive and compensatory damages will satisfy due process" except where a particularly egregious act resulted in a small amount of actual or compensatory damages. The day of the small damages case and the jackpot award of punitive damages may be behind us; the courts will be cautious about allowing any jury award of punitive damages to exceed the compensatory damages by more than a multiple of nine.

The Process Is the Punishment: Extortion by Lawsuit

Effective plaintiff litigators know that the very process of defending a lawsuit is exquisitely expensive. They know that the harder they push, the more intense is the defense effort and the faster the defendant's legal fees are generated. They understand that there is an immediate dollar value to making the pain stop. And they understand that by tacking on a huge claim of damages, spreading the allegations into areas that have nothing to do with the core dispute, and by adding a large number of named individuals, business partners, and licensees as defendants, the action takes on an almost unimaginable weight and importance. The result is that small disputes are magnified completely out of proportion in order to add leverage to the settlement discussions.

This stressful dynamic often comes as a surprise to business defendants on the receiving end of a punitive lawsuit. More than one business executive has wondered whether this is nothing more than legal extortion.

Consider this situation:

> *You own a small retail software business. Recently, a customer in one of your stores was startled when a four-foot tall stacked display of empty nine-inch software boxes was pushed over by an unruly six-year-old customer. The display boxes fell down next to the adult woman customer but did not touch her; she let out a short yelp ("Ohh!") when she saw the boxes falling. You were relieved that the customer was not hit by any of the boxes, that the falling display did not touch her, and that she calmed down immediately. After your store manager assisted her to a chair and gave her a glass of water, she was quite pleasant and apologetic for causing a fuss in the aisle of the store.*
>
> *Weeks later, you receive a letter from an attorney (see Figure 1.1) and enclosed is an official-looking court document titled "Complaint," marked "Draft," and listing as defendants in a lawsuit your company, the name of the software manufacturer on the fallen boxes, the distributor of the software who had stacked the boxes, the name of the six-year-old boy and his parents, the shopping mall in which your store is located, the store manager and assistant manager on duty at the time of the incident, and you and your spouse individually.*

This small mishap—a spill of several small boxes that no doubt startled the customer but did not touch her—has been ratcheted up to a claim of nearly half a million dollars. The attorney knows that an action will be difficult to defend and easy to make him go away—for cash. The attorney no doubt has the matter on a contingency whereby he will receive one-third of any jury award and maybe 50 percent of any settlement, plus his expenses.

FIGURE 1.1: Demand Letter

Dear XYZ Corporation:

This law firm represents Beatrice Bouillabaisse, a single mother of four children residing in Bakersfield, California. Ms. Bouillabaisse has been grievously damaged by the gross negligence of XYZ Corporation and its heartless employees resulting from collapsing display incident in your Fresno store on October 29. We hereby demand compensation for her injuries, her pain and suffering, and her extensive mental anguish.

We estimate that Ms. Bouillabaisse's damages in this matter exceed $475,000. However, Ms. Bouillabaisse is not a litigious person and against our advice has consented to settle this matter immediately for a lump sum payment of $400,000.

If this matter cannot be resolved amicably, we have every intention of filing a court action seeking a judgment in Ms. Bouillabaisse's favor for the full amount of her damages. Please find enclosed a copy of the Complaint we intend to file. Our settlement offer will remain open until the close of business on Wednesday, December 22. If the matter is not settled by that time, we intend to file suit on Thursday, December 23.

We look forward to settling this matter amicably. Please make your check in the amount of $400,000 payable jointly to Ms. Bouillabaisse and my firm, Psuem, Grabbit, & Runn, LLP. Thank you for your cooperation.

Sincerely,

Mickey Finn
Attorney at Law

How does this story make you feel? It is obvious that there was no physical damage to the customer, so the claims will likely be psychological in nature (the "terrorizing" experienced in the store, nightmares, lost sleep, a new fear of software), I suppose. The customer had a moment of surprise and was uninjured, but $475,000 worth?

When you consult your own lawyer, you are told to expect the defense of this lawsuit, if it is filed, will be about $35,000 to $50,000 for the first few months of the action, depending on how aggressive the other side is, and that it could cost you easily $100,000 in legal fees if it goes to trial. That's before you consider the costs in distraction from your business, the time you and your employees will spend in depositions, responding to paperwork, and appearing at trial.

Putting aside the question of coverage by liability insurance, this slight mishap will suddenly cost you a pile of money just to make the ginned-up legal case go away. Or it will cost you even more money in legal fees to defend against the claim, and of course you may lose the case if it goes before an unpredictable jury. You lose either way.

The squeeze on businesses in this situation is excruciating. The soon-to-be-defendant business knows there are no *real* damages in this situation, although in the looking-glass world of the lawsuit, "real" exists only in the eye of the advocate. The store owner knows that this entire situation has been fabricated in order to shake down the business for money. It's extortion, plain and simple. It's not only completely legal, it is pursued in the name of protecting the rights of the individual against the heartless mistakes, carelessness, and mismanagement of business.

Many business owners react emotionally to the injustice of their predicament, insisting that they will not succumb to groundless threats; they will defend the principles of right versus wrong and truth versus falsehood; they will not allow themselves to be a victim of extortion, they will insist that this is the United States of America, and they will say highway robbery in the name of the court system can't be allowed to happen. "Where am I?," a client asked me a few years ago. "I thought this wasn't supposed to happen in America!"

It's not. You're in Lawsuit Hell.

This Is Not Your Father's Lawsuit

T HE PROSECUTION OF LAWSUITS HAS CHANGED. NOT TOO LONG AGO, THE FIL-
ing of a legal action kicked off a rather slow-paced process giving the
parties an opportunity to evaluate the pleadings, review the facts, and
make an informed judgment about the strengths and weaknesses of the
other side's case. Discovery requests tailored to the particular claims in the
Complaint would arrive some weeks after the filing of the suit. The attorneys involved were disinterested professionals, coolly evaluating and
advancing their client's position, showing respect for the process and
humility before the power of the court, which they proudly served as officers of the court.

This reassuring picture went out at about the same time as eight-track
tapes.

It's Fast and Front-Loaded

Statistically, the vast majority of lawsuits never make it to trial. Estimates suggest that 90 to 95 percent of court filings are resolved, dismissed, abandoned, or settled without getting to a final judgment by the finder of fact (either the judge or a jury).

That means that most litigation is used to accomplish something other than a ruling on the facts and the law. In most cases, it is a leveraging prelude to settlement discussions. The fact of the lawsuit becomes the most important bargaining chip, the unthinkably expensive alternative to not settling.

In order to make that alternative to settlement as expensive and unappealing as possible, aggressive plaintiffs' lawyers know to hit the gas pedal hard as soon as they file the Complaint. Immediately after filing the Complaint, attorneys will file a preliminary "summary judgment" motion for a ruling in its favor and serve on the opposition a full set of discovery requests (known as interrogatories, document requests, and requests for admissions). Plaintiff's counsel requests available dates for depositions of various people. Quite suddenly, the defendant's legal team has its hands very full and must begin full scale team litigation. In order to meet the deadlines imposed by court administrators, a team of attorneys is assembled to gather documents, write a formal Answer to the Complaint, meet with the defendant and others named in the action, and draft responses to the discovery requests. Counterclaims are prepared and filed; the defendant's own discovery requests are prepared and filed.

Two weeks into the courthouse proceeding, the defendant's team now has a senior litigation partner, two younger associate lawyers, and two paralegals working nearly full time on the case. Their client is incensed that his organization has been sued and instructs his lawyers to respond in kind, escalating the dispute by a full measure. Have the principals had a chance to discuss the dispute? Is there an alternative to slugging it out like this? There is little time for the attorneys to do anything except meet filing deadlines so that the defendant does not cripple his legal position in the case. The only response the defendant's legal team has is to be reactive.

Down at the law firm, no one can consider draining the swamp while the alligators are snapping.

And snap they do.

Attorney's Fees that Take Your Breath Away

With pride in his voice, one law firm partner confided to me, "Our managing partner now bills $1,000 an hour!"

For a generation, the legal profession has wrestled with how it should bill for legal services. Since the 1960s, using hourly rates for consulting services and litigation defense work and the contingency fees for plaintiff work have grown in acceptance and are nearly universal. An hourly billing arrangement has flexibility. It allows an attorney to handle the unpredictable twists and turns of a particular case without having to set the fee in advance by predicting the amount of work to be involved. But the increasing hourly rate has helped drive legal fees to amazing heights and made the experience of being sued a potentially ruinous one.

Two factors come into play to drive up the fees generated on an hourly rate basis. The first is the business drive of the law firm. Most firms will set goals for their lawyers on the number of billable hours worked in the year, and the goals will be high: 2,100 hours to 2,500 hours will be expected. This compares to the standard articulated by the American Bar Association in the 1950s suggesting that a lawyer's annual billable hours should total about 1,300 hours. To reach the current typical law firm goal of 2,400 hours, the lawyer must have more than 8 billable hours (not administrative work, that's on your own time) each day, 6 days a week for 50 weeks of the year. This is a grueling pace, but it means gross annual figures for a $200/hour associate (employee lawyer) of $500,000. The firm will reward its producers that can match this pace; it will promote a young lawyer to the ranks of the partners after a consistently good showing of such strong billable hours for 7 or 8 years. It will pay the partners a handsome bonus for such high production. Given the pressure that is placed on the almighty number of billable hours, lawyers will take any opportunity to rack up those hours with gusto.

The second factor that pushes up the bill is the reverse motivation of the lawyer. He or she has no motive—financial or otherwise—to curtail a case. The firm is generally not rewarded for a quick resolution of a piece of litigation. Just the opposite. It is punished by the drop-off in the fee stream represented by the case. In an important sense, the lawyer's financial motivation is in direct conflict with his client's interests.

Of course, this dynamic applies only to the defense legal team. Plaintiff lawyers are quite often working on a contingency for a healthy slice of the award or the settlement. Their financial motivation is to drive the case hard and fast and early to demonstrate just how expensive it will be to put off a settlement payment.

Consider the legal team assembled to respond to the case discussed in the last section: a senior litigation partner, two younger associate lawyers, and two paralegals. Let's assume that the senior partner's hourly rate is $365/hour (not everyone is at the $1,000 per hour rate—yet); the associate lawyers are both at $200/hour, and the paralegals are at $100/hour. If the team bills one eight-hour day, it will come to $7,720 *for the day*. Even if the senior lawyer and one of the associates bill only half of the day, the bill for the day will come to $5,460.

The result of these factors is to drive legal expenses to staggering levels. If our fictitious legal team members each bills just eight hours a *week* on the case, it will run up well over $60,000 in legal fees by the end of the second month.

At that point, the case will just be warming up.

Lawsuits Have Changed in the Last 25 Years—Not for the Better

There are a dozen reasons why lawsuits have been advancing as a societal problem for the last 25 years. Many of the changes we have seen in litigation relate to procedural and substantive rules that used to provide a natural brake on the litigation process. Relentlessly, the courts and state legislatures have removed virtually every procedural and substantive standard that previously held lawsuit activities in check.

- *Jurisdiction by long arm.* Where can an American citizen or business expect to be sued? Does a court in a distant state have the jurisdiction to exercise its authority and power over a person or company that has little or no contact with the jurisdiction in which the court sits? The traditional rules of jurisdiction quickly eroded after World War II with a few key Supreme Court decisions and the development of long-arm statutes by the states in the 1960s and 1970s, which essentially opened up a court's jurisdiction to reach any person so long as it did not "offend traditional notions of fair play and substantial justice." No one to this day knows what this means, but the opportunity to sue someone with any flimsy connection to a state has become possible.

- *Pleadings requirements dropped.* Preparing a Complaint to pass judicial scrutiny used to be one of the most difficult hurdles to clear in pursuing a legal claim. A Complaint was required to meet demanding technical standards and had to recite the legal claim with clarity and specificity. Pleadings in the 21st century are far easier, and the courts are far more tolerant of general theories of liability, multiple and alternative claims, unnamed parties, and vague factual allegations to be sharpened after some discovery (often of the fishing expedition variety).

- *Discovery run amuck.* What used to be directly under the supervision of a judge is now almost completely in the province of the litigation attorneys, and what used to be strictly confined to the issues raised in the Complaint is now wide open for classic fishing expeditions. Interrogatories, the formal questions about the situation presented to the other side in writing, are easy to prepare out of published form templates, and they can take hundreds of hours of attorney and management time to answer. Document discovery can require thousands of pages in response. Depositions, those formal interviews by the attorney of one party of a key witness or officer of the other party, had previously been allowed by the courts only where live courtroom testimony would be unavailable or in other rare circumstances. They are now routinely allowed of any number of potential witnesses in the case and can run for days on end.

Discovery abuses are a natural result of the courthouse bottle-neck that so many young lawyers run into. They want to become trial lawyers, but find our public courts crowded with criminal cases and a crush of civil cases, the vast majority of which never make it to trial. The only outlet for their adversarial attorney skills will be in conducting a deposition or arguing discovery disputes and preliminary motions before a judge. It is therefore only natural that more attorney time, effort, and energy would be focused on discovery—and it would be all the more contentious.

- *Spurious junk lawsuits roll on.* The courts system has developed an enormous level of tolerance for lawsuits of dubious substance. Rather than dismiss the extreme or absurd cases, judges allow them to continue in the name of open access to the courts.
- *Awards that make your head spin.* Juries frequently mete out damage awards that rival the gross national product of small countries. The outcome of most cases has become nearly impossible to predict. Extraordinary punitive damages, combined with imaginative compensatory damages, have made the courthouse a roulette wheel of fantastic wealth-building possibilities. For the plaintiff's lawyer, hit the jackpot just once and a lot of failed cases are covered. For defense counsel, the uncertainty of the result has a huge impact on calculations of possible liability exposure in a case.
- *Lawyers now have a large piece of the action.* The lawyer-as-interested-party has become the driving force in a large percentage of lawsuits. Self-interested advocacy has warped the natural interests of the parties and skewed settlement discussions. At what point does an attorney cease representing the interests of his client and start representing his own?

The result is a modern lawsuit that has become toxic, a publicly available money machine driven by self-interested attorneys. Figure 2.1 explores some questions and answers for you to consider as you determine whether you have the foresight and skill to be a modern-day litigator.

FIGURE 2.1: Litigator Qualifying Questions and Answers

Do you have the imagination and the sheer gumption it takes to be a litigating attorney in the 21st century?

I'll give you the facts. You are the lawyer for the complaining party, so you determine who gets sued and who wins how much.

Q: In New York, a drunk driver disregarded traffic signs, lost control of his car, jumped a curb, and hit and injured a pedestrian. Who does the injured pedestrian sue and who wins?

A: He sues the City of New York (of course) claiming the curb was too low. The jury awards $6.3 million to the pedestrian against New York City. (*Newsweek*, December 15, 2003. p. 49)

(That's an easy one to get you warmed up.)

Q: Twenty-nine illegal immigrants sneak across the U.S.-Mexico border into the Cabeza Prieta National Wildlife Refuge north of Yuma, Arizona, one of the most arid and desolate places in North America, and walk for five days in desert temperatures reaching 115 degrees. Eleven people die from exposure and dehydration. Who do the family members sue and for how much?

A: They sue the U.S. government for more than $41 million ($3.75 million for each deceased person), claiming that a recent decision by the Interior Department not to place a water station in the same location as the illegal immigrants perished made the government agency responsible for the tragedy. The case is pending as of this writing in 2004. The federal court has given the plaintiffs additional time to assemble evidence of their claim of government liability. (*Washington Times*, May 17, 2004 by Jerry Separ, "Lawsuit in Death of Aliens Lingers," http://washingtontimes.com/national/20040517-124753-468ar.htm)

Q: A group of fifth grade boys is shooting hoops on a school playground one morning, violating school rules by playing without adult supervision. One of the boys breaks his arm. His mother claims damages because the boy will not be able to play baseball over the summer. Who do you sue and who will pay?

FIGURE 2.1: Litigator Qualifying Questions and Answers, continued

A: You sue the school, of course, but also the parents of all the other boys play-ing ball. The case settled before it went to trial when an insurance company insuring the parents of one of the playmates paid an undisclosed amount to set-tle the claim. (*Newsweek*, December 15, 2003, p. 50)

Q: In jail on suicide watch, an accused serial killer believed by police to have murdered as many as 20 people, one of the murders actually videotaped in his basement, hangs himself from an air vent in his cell, leaving a suicide note. His death is ruled a suicide after investigation. A civil lawsuit is filed by the prison-er's mother seeking $75,000 burial costs and the costs of litigation. Who are the named defendants?

A: The suit named the local county, numerous jail personnel, but also the archi-tects who designed the building (and air vents) and the contractors who built the building and the air vents. (*St. Louis Post-Dispatch*, May 15, 2004, "Prison Builders Sued after Serial Killer's Suicide," www.overlawyered.com/archives/00 1125.html)

The 21st Century Malady

We're All Victims,
Every Pitiful One of Us

MAMMOTH BALEEN WHALES FEED ON ENORMOUS AMOUNTS OF TINY plankton; lawsuits feed on victimhood. We are all victims; it is the idea that drives the crush of lawsuits, and it animates the most extreme legal rulings of our time.

That Victim Thing

Victimhood has taken a solid position in 21st century American culture, and it is struggling to defeat the traditional culture of individual responsibility and industry that has propelled this country to world dominance. In popular culture, television airways are filled with victims telling their stories of failure and abuse at the hands of others. The success of the daily televised

Oprah show, which often focuses on human interest stories, has spawned any number of similar programs highlighting the sad stories of people victimized by their circumstances.

Falling into a victim's frame of mind is the opposite of personal responsibility and accountability. It happens to all of us from time to time. Here's how you can spot the victim's frame of mind:

- You hear yourself blaming someone else for your circumstances.
- You point the finger at others.
- You feel that you do not control your circumstances; "they" do.
- You tend to put off tackling problems in your life or in your working life; you want to wait and see what happens.
- You catch yourself saying, "It's not my job."

This is the defeatist frame of mind of a person who has yielded control and subsequently given up. A victim is content to follow orders, to leave the thinking to others ("Just tell me exactly what you want me to do"), and to spend his time bashing the boss to his co-workers out of frustration.

This attitude is raised to a high art form in the courtroom. Like the teary life story teller on talk show TV blaming a cheating spouse or a nasty family or ungrateful children, the complaining litigant is never responsible for his or her circumstances—it's always something or someone else who is responsible. Of course, proving their victimhood is the very reason for being in court for many plaintiffs (the defendant is responsible and must pay damages).

- The lifelong smoker is not responsible for her cancer. The manufacturer should be responsible because cigarettes are inherently dangerous.
- The sledding father out playing with his kids in the snow is not responsible for his injuries when his sled takes him into a ditch. The city should not have allowed the ditch to be where it was.
- The fired worker is not responsible for his performance on the job. It must be age or race discrimination.
- The teenage girl is not responsible for her eating disorder. It was caused by a verbally abusive PE teacher.

- The McDonald's customer is not responsible for spilling hot coffee in her lap and burning herself while driving a car. The restaurant made the coffee too hot and knew it was dangerous.
- The teenage boy is not responsible the injuries incurred when he dove off a pier into shallow water. It was the lack of a sign warning of the danger.

For victims, the American courtroom is a perfect storm of irresponsibility. Traditional notions of personal choice and responsibility, and assumption of risk, are completely at sea in a court of law. All plaintiffs are presumptive victims in court. Indeed, the defense often feels it has a strategic duty to demonstrate the plaintiff is not a victim at all. We're all victims, and someone else is responsible for ruining our miserable lives. Juries are becoming far more tolerant of this view of life, conditioned by popular culture to identify with the victim, perhaps to see themselves as victims, and to go beyond compensating the victim by actually meting out retribution against the defendant by way of punitive damages.

"If You're a Victim, There Must Be *Someone* We Can Punish"

It follows logically that if a person is a victim, then he has been abused and victimized by *someone* and punishing damages should be awarded against the evil-doer.

Punishment. Now there is a concept that is traditionally alien to the civil courts. Contract law has scrupulously avoided enforcing so much as a "penalty" for a violation of a contract; and tort law (a tort is a civil wrong like an assault and battery) has been careful to leave notions of punishment and retribution to the criminal court system. Civil courts have long acknowledged the English common law tradition of merely righting the civil wrong, of making an injured plaintiff whole, of restoring the wronged person to his condition before the harm was caused by another.

Every time a jury decides to send a message and assess substantial punitive damages, it has traveled way beyond making a victim whole again; it is punishing the defendant. And defendants are being punished in our civil courts without the constitutional protections we afford criminal defendants.

Lawyers as Champions of Victims Everywhere

So much of the abuse that makes a visit to an American court such an odious experience is justified by an appeal close to the American heart: the legal process protects the little guy, providing a place where ordinary people can be heard and receive justice. At its best and in its golden days, that accurately describes the American court system. Senator John Edwards, a North Carolina politician who made millions of dollars in contingency fees suing doctors and hospitals, wrote in *Newsweek*:

> *These days it is fashionable for people to complain that the courts are clogged with frivolous lawsuits, and to dismiss the legal profession as a bastion of greed. In a nation as large as ours, it isn't hard to find an outrageous case here and there. They draw publicity, and it's easy to come away with the impression that the court system is hopelessly broken. . . .People have criticized the jury system, saying juries can't be trusted to consider the facts. I couldn't disagree more. Juries are democracy in action.* (Newsweek, *December 15, 2003, p. 53)*

However, the burgeoning sue-for-profit industry can hardly be dismissed as a problem case "here and there." The American court system has produced an entire generation of lawyers who have been allowed to exploit the weaknesses of the lawsuit system and who have created a sue-for-profit industry that is changing the way Americans live and the way they relate to their neighbors, their service providers, and their co-workers. Politicians and the powerful trial lawyers they represent quite naturally downplay the problem. Creating and representing successful victims in court for profit has become a political and financial force that has become irresistible in our society.

And the more we promote, celebrate, and empathize with the plight of the presumed victim, the worse it will get.

Identifying, understanding, and addressing the victim's frame of mind is an important key to avoiding litigation. As we will see, businesses and professionals can easily see themselves as victimized by their customers and patients (or the legal system or plaintiff lawyers) if a complaint or lawsuit is filed against them. Their giveaway response is that they want nothing to do with the case, saying "let's just leave it to the lawyers." Many would-be plaintiffs see themselves as victims who need acknowledgement of their difficulties and an apology if they think that a mistake was made.

In order to break the litigation cycle and to defend against the sue-for-profit industry, Americans must cure themselves of being victims in any sense and respond effectively to those who would take them to court. The solution lies in building a culture of accountability in your professional or business organization, which is discussed in more detail in later sections of this book.

Waiting for Tort Reform

THE DISCUSSION OF TORT REFORM GETS LIVELY EVERY ELECTION YEAR, AND then it quickly disappears from the forefront of the national agenda. It is an issue that resonates with parts of the electorate. It involves a few very rich and well-entrenched interest groups, particularly corporate interests and the trial lawyers who have made fortunes in the sue-for-profit industry. But the first group typically supports Republican candidates and the second is among the largest contributors to Democratic candidates.

There have been several good tort reform ideas proposed:

- *Cap on damages.* The medical profession has for years pushed for a $250,000 cap on medical damage awards, so far with only modest success. Some caps have been imposed but have largely been circumvented by the courts. The medical profession has seen some truly staggering awards in the past few years. In California, for instance, a jury awarded $59.3 million in 2003 in a suit against a hospital for negligent care contributing to cerebral palsy in a newborn child. (*The Wall Street Journal*, May 18, 2004, p. A14)

- *Strict malpractice liability for bringing frivolous cases.* Even Senator John Edwards suggests that lawyers be more accountable to the courts for bringing frivolous lawsuits; he would impose "tough, mandatory sanctions, with a 'three strikes' penalty." (*Newsweek*, December 15, 2003, p. 53)

- *Separate judicial systems for education and medicine.* This is the most radical—and I think promising—of the ideas proposed. Philip K. Howard, author of *The Death of Common Sense* (Warner Books, 1996), chairs a bipartisan lobbying group, Common Good (www.cgood.org), which has suggested self-contained dispute resolution systems for the educational community and for the medical community. If a complaint about a student's discipline is to be heard, it would not involve local courts; it would go to a review board made up of parents and administrators. If a patient complains about a mistake made by a doctor or hospital, it would go to a board of medical experts. Why, it asks, should the civil law courts be involved in schools or medicine in any way?

- *Procedural changes.* Courts could restrict discovery measures and tighten the rules that lawyers must follow so that discovery is not abused by aggressive lawyering. Another suggestion to counter frivolous lawsuits: require that experts review a medical malpractice claim and certify it has merit before a lawsuit may be filed.

- *"I'm sorry" legislation for doctors.* Already in place in two states (Colorado and Oregon), these laws provide a limited shield for doctors and hospitals who apologize to patients for mistakes made during surgery or other procedures. Many hospitals and doctors, even in states without "I'm Sorry" laws, have turned away from the traditional "defend and deny" approach and have tried being honest and forthright with injured patients. The managing attorney for claims and litigation for Johns Hopkins Hospital was quoted in *The Wall Street Journal* as saying this new forthright and honest approach reduced the hospital's litigation and legal claims expense payments by 30 percent in 2003. (*The Wall Street Journal,* May 18, 2004, p. A14)

• *Cap on punitive damages.* The U.S. Supreme Court tackled the problem of the jackpot punitive damages award in an encouraging 2003 decision that strongly suggested to the courts of the land that any punitive damage award that exceeds compensatory damages by a multiple of double digits would be presumed to violate constitutional standards.

Although these ideas are certainly sensible, tort reform is unlikely to come about in the foreseeable future without a hard political push. There are huge efforts being made by various interest groups, like Common Good, to rein in a civil justice system that is out of kilter. Entrenched interest groups will continue to slug it out. So much money is being made by the trial lawyers and so much of that money is being contributed to sympathetic politicians that I do not expect dramatic changes in the civil courts system in the decade ahead.

As frustrating as it may be to see our society play politics with a troubled institution, we have a challenge that is far more immediate and compelling: avoiding the expense, uncertainty, and absurdity of the courthouse *today.*

Yes, Something CAN Be Done Now!

T HIS BRIEF REVIEW OF THE STATE OF THE AMERICAN SUE-FOR-PROFIT INDUSTRY is discouraging. An exemplary legal system is being abused by the very officers of the court, as attorneys are called, who are entrusted with its smooth and just operation. Judges have let loose the controls on the litigation process. Legislatures have knocked down the rules that protected our privacy and the dignity of the system. There are virtually no checks on the ability of a plaintiff and his attorney to bring ruinous expense to the doorstep of any individual or business in the country. Any hope of tort reform is strangled by the conflict among politically powerful interest groups in our society. There is no relief in sight.

I strongly believe that businesses and individuals have no choice but to take steps to protect themselves as effectively as possible in this environment.

There is much that can be done now. We must take the legal system as it is and build the best defenses possible. While it may not be possible to guarantee you will never be pulled into the courts system, it is certainly possible to improve the odds in your favor. With the right tools, skills, and attitude about conflicts and accountability either in your personal life or in the life of your organization, you can dramatically lower the risks of ruinous exposure to a legal system raging out of control.

Asserting Your Real Interests—Beyond Winning a Lawsuit

The mark of a good dispute resolution procedure is that it addresses the real interests of the parties to the dispute. The mark of a *great* procedure is its flexibility to accommodate those interests in the resolution of the dispute. A courtroom lawsuit does not fare well by this measure. The interests of the parties are usually recast entirely for maximum advocacy impact as extreme, inflexible positions and are generally reduced to one-dimensional money damages.

The key to effective conflict resolution is the expression and exploration of the parties' *real interests*. This key insight has nothing to do with winning lawsuits; it goes well beyond that to a basic understanding of the nature of disputes between people.

It is necessary to look beyond positions to get at real interests.

Resolving Conflicts Can Improve Relationships

Now here is a notion people never associate with the outcome of a lawsuit—improving the relationship between the disputants. In fact, resolving a dispute, really resolving it, can significantly improve the business or personal relationship you have with the other side. This happens quite naturally because of the human dynamic of working through and around real interests.

If there is one lesson and skill I hope you develop as a result of reading this book, it is recognizing that an articulated position is merely a position; it is a veil, a mask whose job it is to hide real interests and present a calculated vision of the visage underneath. The real work in conflict resolution in all circumstances is to see behind the mask. Here are a few examples where a party's *real* interest is not immediately apparent.

- A college professor demands an unusually high raise in salary, threatening the dean with immediately leaving the school if she doesn't get it. After some patient discussion, the Dean learns her real interest: she wants more professional recognition of her work and has been bitterly disappointed at being left off a list of faculty receiving awards for their work—for the fourth year in a row.

- Parents of a child seriously hurt in a school sporting event demand millions in a lawsuit. Their real interests are taking care of their son and making sure that other children are not hurt by the same conditions. They need to be convinced that the school is accountable and responsive to the injury.

- A surgery patient goes through a simple surgical procedure and comes out with serious complications because of a mistake by the anesthesiologist. He makes a full recovery but visits the family lawyer to discuss some sort of compensation for his difficulties. A suit is prepared demanding millions; but his real interests are not reflected in any effort to ruin the career of a good doctor who made a mistake or the monetary damages claimed. They are more personal. He wants a sincere apology, help getting back on his feet at his job, and a training program put in place at the hospital that will prevent similar mistakes from happening again. When these things do not happen, he gets angry and files the suit.

When a sales representative responds to a buyer's request for a lower price by countering with a longer purchase commitment, a deal can be made. Each party has real interests that are met by lower price on one side and longer purchasing commitment on the other. Real interests are generally revealed after people exchange information about themselves, establish a level of trust or at least understanding, and fashion a resolution that meets those real needs.

A lawsuit is the ultimate mask of real interests. It is nothing more than a lawyer's collection of demands and threats and extreme positions. Other dispute resolution tools—negotiation, arbitration, mediation, or other means of alternate dispute resolution—are certainly superior to going to court.

The best defense against the lawsuit, of course, is to prevent it from being filed in the first place. There are a few keys to careful lawsuit avoidance:

- Building accountability into the culture of your organization.
- Being willing to step outside of the constrictions imposed by lawyers.
- Using alternate dispute resolution tools to your advantage.
- Being willing to move quickly to intervene in a growing dispute.
- Improving the conflict management skills of those on your management team.

Taking Control of Your Destiny

I have seen too many professionals and business people respond to being sued by yielding all decision-making and resolution initiatives to the lawyers, skilled professionals no doubt, and leaving resolution of the dispute to the litigation process. Many do that because they don't know they have choices, because they don't realize that there might be a better way to address the dispute, and because they don't understand the limitations under which most attorneys work.

I am a strong believer in the value of a different approach, a bold direct stroke that keeps the business people exploring resolution, and keeps alive the possibility that the parties can break out of the litigation headlock and get to their real interests.

PART II

Conflict Resolution Skills

Laying the Groundwork to
Avoid Costly Disputes

Litigant: A person about to give up his skin for
the hope of retaining his bones.
—AMBROSE BIERCE

AT THE BEGINNING OF EVERY LAWSUIT OR POTENTIAL LAWSUIT IS A lost opportunity to resolve a basic dispute. Roll back the video tape of any situation that comes to a head in a civil court of law, and you will find a moment of conception that features a serious communication failure complicated by a toxic cocktail of pride, bullheadedness, fear, greed, anger, and ego.

As things escalate and lawyers get involved, the conflict compounds and becomes progressively harder to resolve. Positions harden (even though interests are unchanged), threats are thrown across the widening chasm, and serious miscalculations set in. Communications are cut off by the lawyers, and along the way a claim is filed in a courtroom.

What can we do to head off this seemly inevitable progression? If we could go back to the magic moment of conflict escalation, what could we have said or done to diffuse the situation and avoid the eventual lawsuit? Consider how our communications can be effective when a conflict flares up.

Six Conflict Resolution Techniques That Improve Relationships

T HE STRESS BROUGHT ON BY A DISPUTE CAUSES MANY OF US TO SHUT DOWN our basic communications skills. We become defensive or argumentative, or simply tongue tied. Sometimes, it seems, anything we say only makes matters worse. Yet we know that the only reasonable solution is to confront the people involved. Yikes.

I have boiled this whole area down to six steps. Master these basic concepts and you will improve your conflict resolution skills exponentially.

Step 1: We're All in This Together

Here's rule one when working on a conflict:

It's "We"—Not You *vs.* Me

Watch your words carefully. Do not use adversarial terms and never be accusatory. Your goal is to metaphorically slide around the table to stand next to the person who is in conflict with you. It is not "Your problem, you jerk." It's "our conflict," "our new project," or " our conflict to tackle together."

Best Approach

> *James, you and I have not really talked about the Moneypenny account flap, and I have been worried that our working relationship has suffered from our lack of communication. I was hurt by your attitude at the staff meeting last week. You and I have a challenge here—and I feel a bit awkward about it. It's something of an odd job, but I'm sure we can work on it together.*

Don't Say

> *Look, James, you were a real jerk in last week's meeting on the Moneypenny account. You actually accused me in from of the entire team of undermining our objectives and nearly losing the account. You went out of your way to make me mad! I think you've got a real problem. I've had it up to here with your irresponsible shenanigans, but Quincy asked me to see if we can smooth things over between us. What do you want to do?*

Notice the use of "I"feelings in the first example, and the way the situation becomes "our challenge" that "we" can work on "together." The second example is sure to inflame the problem.

Step 2: Re-Frame the Conflict

Remind the other person that you have a relationship that is not defined by this conflict. In fact, the conflict is only the smallest part of your relationship, and it's certainly not the best part.

This lends immediate perspective to the dispute you are resolving. It invites both people to think back to stronger days they have in common and then to think about recreating that success in the future. Listen to this example:

> *Look, Marcie, we have worked on the same production team for more than two years, and together we have produced some of the finest sprocket designs in the entire history of the company. Do you remember when you and Jack and I won the Cobham Award last year? We were invincible! With a little teamwork, we'll work through our conflict over the Littlehill project. I'm sure of it. I want us to get back to our strong working partnership, and I hope you feel the same way.*

Reach back in time and find stronger ground. Remind the other person of what first brought you together, what worked, and how you felt about it. This has the effect of shrinking the conflict and allowing both sides to find comfortable ground from which to address your mutual new challenge.

The same dynamic will apply between organizations working through a conflict. Remind the other side about the depth of the relationship between the businesses over the years, the people from one company who now work for the other, the community projects you have both supported, the fun you have shared at industry conferences, your past mutual successes.

If you have no long history with the other side, consider highlighting the commitment that you have both made to be in your situation. In the case of new neighbors for example, each has invested heavily to own the adjoining property and each looks forward to many years of quiet enjoyment and goodwill in the neighborhood. The trick is to put the conflict into a larger frame, reminding the parties they have a lot at stake in the successful outcome of the conflict.

The very fact of the larger frame, affirming your successful history or mutual commitment, will inevitably improve your relationship, and certainly improve your odds of resolving the conflict between you.

Step 3: Gentle Confrontation

I surprise clients in our seminars when I insist that, despite this age of road rage and hair-on-fire political discourse, we need MORE—not less—confrontation in our society. Confrontation is pivotal in successful conflict resolution, but I don't mean confrontation that is intimidating or threatening. I mean a gentler, more inquisitive confrontation by which the two sides can clarify their perceptions of the situation and share their views of the conflict.

This is accomplished with the use of nonthreatening questioning and active listening, two essential skills in conflict resolution.

Example

> *Tony, would you please tell me your perception of this problem?*
> *I want to make sure I understand the situation as you see it.*

Notice that this question contains useful phrases, "your perception of the problem" and "the situation as you see it." These questions acknowledge the unique perspective everyone brings to a conflict, with no suggestion that the other person is "wrong" in any way. They create an opportunity for the other person to talk openly about what has occurred from his or her perspective. No one can challenge a person's perceptions.

Your objective here is to get perceptions out on the table, to clarify and refine them until you and the other person have a crystal clear understanding of one another's perceptions of the conflict.

Active Listening

Active listening is a dying art. It must be studied and practiced, and it is difficult to do well for any sustained period of time, harder by far than talking for the same period of time. It is focused, undistracted, and concentrated. You look the other person in the eye; you're not watching the room. You don't interrupt. You are asking question to clarify your understanding, and mirroring statements made so that the other person understands that you have received the message. You take notes. You show a serious interest in the other person's experience and perceptions.

Active listening is the most effective expression of *compassion.* It is the expression of compassion that resolves disputes. When listening actively,

- Find a place with no distractions.
- Face the other person and listen intently.
- Take notes.
- Maintain eye contact.
- Be aware of your (and their) facial expressions and body language.
- Mirror and summarize.
- Express sincere empathy for the other side's situation.
- Ask questions. Then ask more questions.

This is also the occasion where you should clarify *your* perceptions of the situation. This is a shared process, after all.

Should you express your emotions? Yes, if offered carefully so that they do not trigger guilt or become accusatory. You must continue to be part owner of the conflict, as illustrated below.

> *George, I've got to tell you that I was really angry after our staff meeting on Monday, and you were part of the reason for my anger. I've calmed down now, but I still feel resentful about the comments you and Paul made about our team's performance last month. Maybe I misunderstood what was going on. Could we spend a few minutes and work through it so that I understand your perception of the situation?"*

Be prepared in any conflict resolution situation for tempers to flare. Be in a frame of mind that is not challenged by such a show of emotion. Let it go. Look beyond it. Your patience and calm persistence in the face of a temper flare up will do more to set the tone that anything else you can do or say.

Step 4: Looking Beyond Positions

Your questioning and active listening has an important objective in this dispute resolution: to identify the other side's needs and, ultimately, to locate your overlapping shared needs.

Progression Toward Resolution

Positions ➤ *Interests* ➤ *Mutual Benefits*

Wants ➤ *Needs* ➤ *Shared Needs*

Recognizing shared needs is the very fabric of relationships, personal and institutional.

The only way to get past each of these roadblocks is through effective questions and a purposeful give and take. Along the way, a conflict manager should be looking for small stepping stones to success, achievable steps toward resolution that will allow the parties to move ahead.

Read through the following questions to see what I mean.

Questions to Clarify Perceptions and Gain Information

- I think I understand. Can you give me an example?
- Tell me more about _____.
- I'm still not clear, what exactly did the foreman say about the accident?
- Can you describe what happened at the sales presentation in some more detail?

Questions to Identify Interests

- What is important to you in this situation?
- Can you help me understand *why* that is important to you?
- What things do you need most?
- What is it that you need our relationship to provide?
- What can we do together in this conflict process that will strengthen our relationship?

Questions to Generate Options, Stepping-Stones

- What would work for you on this point?

- What could we do together to tackle this issue?
- What would make my idea work better for you?
- Is this solution realistic?
- Is there some way we could meet your need *and* mine?

Questions Regarding Consequences

- If we can't work this out, what other options do you have?
- If we put that idea in place and then [XX] happens, then what?

Questions Confirming Agreement Terms

- Is there anything we left out?
- Are you comfortable with this wording?
- Is there any aspect of our agreement that concerns you?
- Can you live with this from today on?

Tips for Questions

"Why" questions can make some people defensive. It may sound like you are prying for information they do not want to offer voluntarily. Substitute "what" for "why" when you can.

Why Question

"Why didn't you pay the rent?"

What Question

"What made it difficult for you to meet September's rent payment?"

The biggest mistake you can make in this process is to make assumptions about the perceptions and needs of the other person. *Never assume.* Ask the other person about his/her perceptions and needs, and go from there. The articulation of those views and perceptions will point the way to the shared needs of your relationship.

Step 5: Finding Mutually Beneficial Solutions

Now that the issues are identified and perceptions clarified, you want to explore resolutions that address your shared needs and offer benefits to all parties involved. Start with small stepping stones toward resolution, manageable measures that you know will be successful.

- *Generate options.* The most promising options will be based on the real interests you can identify in your discussion. Look for opportunities to arrive at a win-win solution.
- *Use the pivotal word "if" in the give and take about solutions.* "Sure I can do that for you, IF you are willing to do this for me."
- *Make small concessions.*
- *Review the negotiation basics in Chapter 8.*

The last yard is the hardest. In many dispute settlement negotiations, the final point can be the most difficult. It becomes symbolic of the entire dispute in the minds of some disputants, and they dig in and insist on making no more concessions. They want to force a symbolic victory in the struggle. You may want to offer to split the difference or decline the concession entirely and keep negotiating, but if it is a relatively small point, consider being generous and giving up the last point. In my experience, you secure a larger measure of goodwill and future consideration with a small concession to conclude the settlement.

Step 6: Putting the Settlement in Writing

Whether you are resolving a small conflict with an office mate or a serious dispute that could lead to expensive litigation, an agreed upon resolution should be put in writing.

A settlement of litigation will necessarily involve preparation of settlement papers by your legal counsel addressing the issues necessary to dispose of the lawsuit and also articulating the stepping-stones and other terms agreed on in the resolution process.

The resolution of other disputes may not actually require such a formal writing, but in my experience writing down the understanding of the disputing parties will always assist in keeping the newly strengthened relationship on solid ground. The terms of that agreement will replace the conflicting demands that were made by both sides, so their clarity is of utmost importance.

Figure 6.1 shows a simple format that should convey the parties intent and state in positive terms what was agreed on.

FIGURE 6.1: Settlement Checklist

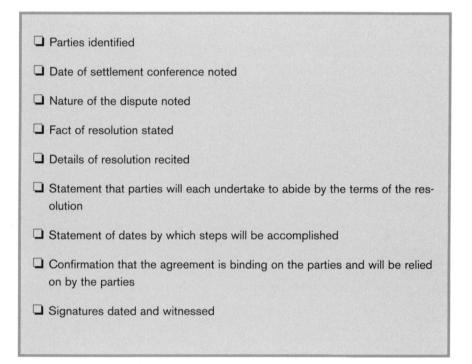

❑ Parties identified

❑ Date of settlement conference noted

❑ Nature of the dispute noted

❑ Fact of resolution stated

❑ Details of resolution recited

❑ Statement that parties will each undertake to abide by the terms of the resolution

❑ Statement of dates by which steps will be accomplished

❑ Confirmation that the agreement is binding on the parties and will be relied on by the parties

❑ Signatures dated and witnessed

Communication
to Avoid
Lawsuits

APPLYING THE PRINCIPLES OF CONFLICT RESOLUTION DISCUSSED IN THE LAST chapter can be difficult when tempers are flaring and wills are pitted one against another. At what point should a lawyer be called into a dispute, and how should you respond when you receive a threatening letter from a lawyer?

Project Accountability

So many lawsuits result from a breakdown of communication. When a person feels hurt or aggrieved for some reason, he or she wants to see that the grievance is felt, understood, and fully addressed. When that doesn't happen, the natural responses are frustration, anger, and a feeling of powerlessness. Here is a case in point. An article in *Lawyers Weekly USA* ("The National Newspaper for Small Law Firms") on April 12, 2004, p. 1, carried the headline "High School Athlete Nets $1.47M in Suit Over Verbally Abusive Coach," and the boxed leader stated, "Small Firm Victory." The article reports on a New Jersey lawsuit in which the plaintiff was an overweight high school girl who received verbal abuse from her basketball coach and claimed that this caused her to develop a serious eating disorder and other problems. The jury awarded her $1.47 million against the school district and the coach. Toward the end of the article, there is the accountability issue. "[The girl's] attorneys said the case would never have gone to court if [the coach] had simply apologized for his behavior." Whether or not this statement is true, it underscores the importance of communication in a lawsuit setting and the significance of accountability, or lack of accountability, as a motivator for so many lawsuits.

The plaintiff's comments are telling: "It was just like vindication," she was quoted as saying. "I wanted to jump up and hug the jury. I felt like, man, somebody finally listened and heard my story and believed me."

But what if the school board had responded to the complaints with concern and had admonished the coach? If the coach had met with the girl and her family and apologized for losing his temper and yelling at her? If the school board had responded creatively, by putting in place a teacher/coach complaint evaluation system to give professional reports to school principals? It is quite possible the girl and her family would have felt that they had been heard and the board was handling the situation responsibly by being accountable for the actions of its employees.

In order to steer away from court, your communications in the face of any sort of complaint—no matter how specious it may be—should project full accountability. The traditional response, to deny any allegation of liability, may still be appropriate, but only in the context of the company's accountability.

Figure 7.1 is an example of a response to a complaint submitted to a nursing home director alleging inadequate care of an elderly resident of the home.

FIGURE 7.1: Response to a Complaint

Dear Mr. Dogsbody:

We have received you letter of June 7 regarding the care your mother is receiving in our Springfield nursing home facility. We are naturally concerned about the quality of care our residents receive, and we take great pride in having received professional awards for the quality of the care offered in the Springfield facility.

We understand that you are concerned about sores that have appeared on your mother's legs, and we are taking immediate action to look into her situation. Mrs. Dogsbody has been a resident at our Springfield facility for nearly six years now, and the nursing staff has come to know your mother quite well and takes a special interest in her well-being. They tell me they enjoy her wry sense of humor. After our medical team completes its evaluation of your mother's condition, which will take us two to three days, we will be in touch with you to discuss our findings and our staff's recommendations for Mrs. Dogsbody's treatment and care. I know from my personal discussions with Mrs. Dogsbody and our staff nurses that your mother is fighting a number of serious health problems, including Alzheimer's disease, diabetes, anemia, hypertension, and the consequences of two strokes.

You suggest in your letter that the sores have occurred because our facility has been understaffed and we have not turned Mrs. Dogsbody in bed with sufficient frequency. We certainly hope this is not the case, but we will address the situation immediately if our care in any way contributes your mother's medical difficulties.

We will be in touch with you again in a few days after we receive the professional evaluation of Mrs. Dogsbody's condition and care. Perhaps we could schedule a meeting with you and your mother to go over our findings and plan of action. I will call you toward the end of this week to schedule a meeting at your convenience.

Very truly yours,

Jeremiah Katz
Director

This letter conveys a clear message of accountability. It tells Dogsbody that his concerns have been heard and understood and that the care facility is responding to them in a responsible fashion. This letter cannot and should not appear on an attorney's letterhead. It is far more believable and sincere coming from the people directly responsible for the situation. As a lawyer, I have ghostwritten hundreds of letters for my clients to be sent out on the clients' letterhead. Strategically, I have found that the appearance of an attorney's letterhead just draws in the other side's attorney and dramatically shifts the dispute from a manageable business matter into a table-thumping legal exercise.

What if the complaint letter arrives on an attorney's letterhead? In many circumstances, I have advised clients to send a brief note to the lawyer giving my contact information as the company's legal counsel and then to write a direct, personal response to the person behind the complaint. The lesson: Let lawyers talk to lawyers, but never assume that just because a lawyer is in the picture that all communication between the principals must stop.

B2B Is Always Better than A2A

There are few developments in the life of a dispute like attorney involvement. I am a firm believer that individuals, professionals, and business people should keep attorneys out of the picture *as long as possible*. If you understand how limited is the thinking, training, and experience of most attorneys, and the disruptive impact that attorneys have on a dispute, you would understand why I have reached that conclusion.

Your typical attorney has been trained in the power of advocacy and the intimidation of the court system. He sees his role as that of a kind of royal intimidator, one who understands the court system and who is in a position to arrogantly threaten to resort to that court system. As advocates, lawyers see themselves as having the essential function in the judicial process of articulating their clients' best arguments as they struggle for a decision in their favor by a judge or jury. "Best" arguments tend to be rather extreme. Most lawyers will tell you that they prefer to set out an extreme position because it assists when it comes time to resolve the dispute, either by settlement or a judge/jury decision.

Extreme, extended arguments, in other words, have an important place in the American judicial system. That's what makes horse races in a court; that is how the game is played there.

Consider the lawyer who displays this tendency in his opening argument to a jury in a patent case:

> *This is a case where the other side will deny everything. It is like the gardener who goes to his neighbor and says, "Your goat got into my garden and ate all my vegetables, and I'd like you to make it right." The neighbor, a lawyer by training, says, "You don't own a garden, and, by the way, I don't own a goat. But if I did, I certainly would not let it near your property, and if I wanted to let a goat near your property, I would certainly ask your permission first."*

Aggressive lawyers will deny the air we breathe and make you prove its existence. Extreme positioning is the nature of courtroom argumentation. Admit nothing; deny every conclusive statement; and make the other side prove every single aspect of the case. The opponent answers by articulating his best case, his own extreme position, and the court makes its judgment.

Attorneys are not trained in the businesses or the various professions they are attacking or defending. They are generally not trained in conflict resolution or in alternate dispute resolution. They tend not to think creatively about dispute resolution because they are neither paid nor trained to do so. They know only the law and the process of the American lawsuit. When your one tool is a hammer, most of the world begins to look like a nail.

Lawyers bring this extreme and argumentative mindset to disputes outside the courtroom, and the effect is always polarizing. They don't bring people together; just the opposite is true. They also change the dispute dynamic by bringing to litigation an express or tacit threat of escalating the dispute.

The most disruptive aspect of attorney involvement, however, is removal of the principals of the dispute from communication with one another. Some people who are uncomfortable in a conflict situation are relieved to hand off to attorneys the responsibility for communicating with increasingly hostile counterparts; and some attorneys insist that they be the only point of communication so that there is no confusion about positions taken or undercutting concessions made. Of course, if one side brings in a lawyer, the other side will do the same. After all, it makes sense that lawyers should be communicating only with lawyers. In fact, legal ethics require that a lawyer not communicate directly with a non-lawyer opponent if that opponent has indicated it is represented by legal counsel. The result is predictable: the dispute falls into the hands of people who have no interest in seeing it resolved efficiently and are singularly well-equipped by training and experience to present the dispute only to a court of law.

It also creates a classic communications nightmare: principals talking to their lawyers who filter comments and talk to the other side's lawyers, who in turn filter the message and talk to their own clients. Any chance of the parties actually communicating on the issues at hand quickly fades away.

This is not conflict resolution at all—it's conflict avoidance.

Early Intervention

Dispute intervention is one of the most effective tools you can use to interrupt the nonproductive death grip that too many attorneys have on disputes. If a dispute is put into the hands of legal counsel and you see it going in the wrong direction, which is to say toward court, the principals or an outside professional must take immediate steps to intervene and restart communication between the principals, those who own the dispute.

An intervention, conducted thoughtfully, will bring together the principals, and unavoidably their attorneys, for direct discussions about the dispute. The principals may want to decide not to have attorneys at the meeting. Often, more can be accomplished without them in the room. The topics of discussion should include not only the issues to be resolved but the process by which they will be addressed. Should a series of meetings be planned for negotiating on the issues? Should the sides hire a mediator to assist in the negotiating? Does the dispute lend itself to a mini-trial or arbitration? Why assume that the only way to resolve the dispute is by going to court?

Expect resistance from the lawyers. They will see it as nothing more than a poorly timed settlement conference that could somehow weaken their client's legal position.

"My Lawyer Can Beat Up Your Lawyer"

Businesspeople in particular make a frequent miscalculation about litigation. They too often assume that an opponent who is smaller and has fewer resources to waste on a lawsuit will not put up a legal fight. While it is true that large law firms and their wealthy clients can increase the pace and expense of a lawsuit against a less-moneyed opponent, their usual reaction if opposed is surprise that a smaller opponent and her lawyers can put up a sustained effort and even hit back hard.

It is always a miscalculation to think that filing a lawsuit will so shock and awe an opponent that she will surrender. Lawyers are far too plentiful and far too willing to work on contingency or reduced, deferred fees for that to happen. A filed lawsuit will almost always be met with counter-claims and a diligent effort to engage fully in the wasteful pursuits of the case.

The Exact Moment When Lawsuits Happen

Every lawsuit is the culmination of a series of events and exchanges, of calculations and miscalculations, of a struggle of wills. In an important sense, the filing of a lawsuit is an admission of failure. The parties in the dispute reach the point where they no longer believe that they can find a resolution of the dispute by their own hand. They leave it to the lawyers, and the lawyers in turn take it to a court for decision. The moment when one party to a dispute yields direct involvement and puts the dispute into the hands of the lawyers is the moment when the lawsuit happens. The lawyers may continue to negotiate or exchange threats for a while before one of them files the legal action, but the real moment of creation of the lawsuit is the magic point where one of the disputants turns his back on finding a direct, private solution.

It is important to understand that people can intervene and effectively defer that moment by teaching the disputants what they need to know about conflict resolution techniques, impressing on them the shortcomings of a public court battle, exploring the alternative resolution tools available, and confirming the importance of accountability in their continuing discussions.

Essential Negotiation Skills

E VEN IF YOU ARE NOT THE WORLD'S GREATEST NEGOTIATOR, YOU HAD BETTER be familiar with the basic process and the principles of negotiating in order to effectively avoid the courthouse. Much of the work of avoiding lawsuits involves a careful give and take that follows the precepts of any productive negotiation. The dispute context places its own unique demands on the negotiators.

Negotiating So Both Sides Can Win

The overall objective of a mutually satisfying negotiation is to arrange for both sides to walk away from the table feeling that they have succeeded in achieving the best terms possible given the circumstances. Both sides can win, a jarring concept in a judicial contest where each side is pressing its advantage to prevail in court. A win-win outcome involves each side learning quite a bit about the needs and desires of the other side. If a negotiator is well informed about the interests of his counterpart, he can look for the particular needs of the other side, those negotiating points that have high value to them and low cost to him.

The challenges of negotiating a legal dispute are aggravating. If lawyers become involved, they immediately separate the parties, forcing the principals to communicate only through their representatives. This can paralyze negotiation efforts. The other typical result of lawyer involvement, as we have discussed, is that they reduce the interests and needs of the parties to a single dimension: money. Claims of compensatory damages and punitive damages are measured only in dollars, limiting all possible solutions to dollars. The dispute becomes a one-dimensional power struggle for money, with only one question: how much money will one party pay to the other to make the lawsuit go away? And of course, the lawyers are inflicting as much financial pain as possible in the conduct of the lawsuit. No wonder it feels like extortion. The leverage being pressed by the litigators has nothing to do with the merits of the situation. The pressure to settle is about financial cost of the litigation process, the relative merits of the allegations, not the real issues in dispute that brought about the lawsuit.

Negotiating Principle: Aim Above Your Target

This is probably one of the biggest mistakes made by poor negotiators: they start with an opening position that is too low. In fact, most people—most Americans anyway—are inclined to open in a negotiation with a position they feel is fair to both sides, one they can justify and feel comfortable defending. It is often the position they would like to end up in; it is their target position. They articulate their position and launch into why it is fair and fully justified.

Then what happens? The other side listens impassively and then starts pressing for concessions, and with each concession, the position looks less and less attractive. The result is predictable: the negotiator's position is pulled lower and lower so that the only way out is to either accept a result that is far lower than expected or walk away from the table.

The answer is to start with an aggressive opening position, shooting high, well above your target position. In every negotiation, you should prepare in advance a clear idea of your (aggressive) opening position, the position where you would like to end up (your target position), and your bottom line, walk away limit (the point below which it is not in your interests to pursue the negotiation any further). Armed with these goals and targets in advance, you will not be forced to make decisions in the heat of a negotiating exchange that you have not thought out carefully.

One practical reason for starting high is so that you have room to make concessions, to give up something in your position. Give and take is essential to a successful negotiation; both sides showing their good faith by agreeing to concessions in their position, showing a willingness to meet in the middle ground. Another practical advantage is that the other side may come back and be willing to settle at a level above your target position.

Negotiating Principle: Say *Yes* Whenever Possible

A high opener allows you to say "yes" when your counterpart asks you for something. We all like to hear *yes* in our dealings with other people; it is music to the ears. There is nothing as discouraging as asking your counterpart for an important concession and be flatly told "no."

Good negotiators will rarely answer *no*; they will consider the request thoughtfully, evaluate it on its merits, and if it is something within the realm of possibility, invariably answer, "Yes, I might be able to give you that point IF you'll do this for me. . . ." Using the big IF in negotiating is an important habit to develop. It allows you to say *yes*, but it is always qualified. It says, "I am willing to give on this point, but I want you to give something back to me for it." Use the big IF and make no "free" concessions.

Negotiating Principle: Make Small Concessions and Watch Your Concession Patterns

Resist the temptation to make a large concession in your position, hoping that it will be seen as generous and signaling the end of the negotiating. A large leap in your concessions rarely sends such a signal. In fact just the opposite signal will be sent; the other side will think, "I'll just hold tight and maybe he'll do it again."

Concession patterns tell a lot to the other side; they send a most definite signal because actions always speak louder than words. You want to control that signal as best you can. Here is the point of sending a signal: you want to convey to your opponent that with smaller and smaller concessions, you are approaching your bottom line—when, in fact, you are approaching your target position. You have to be convincing, and you must be conservative and clear with your concessions. Rush too fast to your target position and your opponent will think there is more you can give. Give the wrong pattern of concessions and your opponent will not be convinced you are approaching a limit.

Take a look at Figure 8.1, the five concession patterns, and think about how the other side would respond to them in the negotiation. Your opening position is 300, your target is 200, and your bottom line position is 100. You can give away the 100 points (between your opening position and your target) in up to five concessions steps. Remember, your objective is to convince the other side that as you approach the 200 level you are running hard into your bottom line position, and the other side is getting the best deal possible from you.

FIGURE 8.1: Five Concession Patterns

Pattern	Concession A	Concession B	Concession C	Concession D	Concession E	Total Concessions
1	0	0	0	0	100	100
2	20	20	20	20	20	100
3	5	10	15	25	45	100
4	100	0	0	0	0	100
5	45	25	15	10	5	100

Pattern 1

You stonewall in marathon negotiation sessions, refusing to give an inch on your opening position of 300. You spend total energies arguing to explain and justify your opening position. The other side starts to lose interest, and you decide to make one huge last minute concession, hoping they will think you are making your one time take-it or leave-it grand gesture. What does the other side think? "Now we are finally making some progress! That's a good first step, even though we had to work hard for it. Surely there are more generous concessions to come."

Pattern 2

You make a series of equal concessions, but there is no signal that you are getting close to anything. The other side will want you to keep going until you get tired of yielding 20 points on each exchange. "Let me get comfortable, and clear my schedule," they will think, "I could go all day at this rate."

Pattern 3

This is a negotiator's nightmare pattern. If you make increasingly larger concessions, you are creating expectations that you will not be able to meet, and it will be very difficult to bring the negotiation to a successful close.

Pattern 4

One large concession and then stonewall. Your opponents are hanging on, hoping that you will make another whopping concession.

Pattern 5

This sends a clear signal, and is by far the best of the concession patterns. The pattern of concessions shows that you are growing tougher and less generous as you approach the 200 level. Your opponent will see the smaller concessions and will see where you are headed, convinced that you are arriving at your bottom line and have nothing more to give.

Negotiating is addictive. Once you get a feel for the strong opening/target/bottom line structure and the basic rules of the give and take of negotiation, you will approach so many more transactions, and, yes, disputes with a greater confidence. Exercise some caution, though, when you are heading into unfamiliar waters.

Negotiating Principle: More Give and Take

Setting an aggressive opener without sufficient information about the range of possibilities can be a problem. You want to shoot high but remain in a range of reasonability. You want to deliver your opener with a straight face, so it had better be within the range of reasonability. Fall out of the range of what is reasonable, and it could project that you are not negotiating in good faith. You need information to know where that range is. Here's an example.

> Imagine we are negotiating the purchase of a small statue for the garden with an antiques dealer. As it turns out, this is exactly the piece you have been seeking for years; it is a copy of the statue in you parents' garden while you were growing up. Your heart leaps in your throat when you see it, and you are determined not to leave the shop without it.
>
> The price tag on the statue says $199. You determine that your budget could handle a $160 purchase, and so, savvy negotiator that you are, you approach the shop owner with a casual air. "I notice that you have an old garden statue over there with some weather damage and a chipped knee cap. Too bad it's all beat-up, or it would be worth close to the $199 price. I'll tell you what I'll do. I will pay you $145 for the statue; that's a fair price given the damage and the repairs I'll have to make." You are so smooth, and such a damn fine negotiator even you can't believe it.
>
> You have made a fair opener; it is aggressive, you think, without being completely out of the ballpark. You hold your breath. You're sure he's going to tell you to forget it, or come back with a counter offer that pushes you well above your budget.
>
> The shop owner gives a surprising reply, "Did you say $145? You've got it, sport. Make your check out to Ajax Clutter Box Inc. please. Do you need any help getting it to your car?"

How does that make you feel? You realize instantly that you must have made a mistake with your opening offer. You kick yourself as you hand over your credit card; you are convinced you could have done much better. "This isn't a deal at all," you mutter to yourself. "There must be something wrong with the statue that I can't see, a crack or some internal damage that has been covered over. And every time you look at that statue, even though you will be pleased to have it, a small voice in your ear will always remind you that you could have had a better deal if you had been a more effective negotiator.

Change the shop owner's response in a second scenario. If he had wanted his customer to feel better about the transaction, he would have responded to the opening offer with a counteroffer. "That's pretty low figure for that piece, and I don't want to lose money on it. But it does have a bit of weather damage. I suppose I could come down to $180." After more conversation and a couple more concessions you settle on a price of $165. Now how do you feel? You are on top of the world! A garden statue with such wonderful sentimental value, and a great deal that you negotiated like a pro! You may have paid more than you would have in the first scenario, but it is a far more satisfying transaction. The negotiation actually enhanced the value of the item in question.

Negotiating Principle: Dropping the Hammer

In the first scenario, two mistakes were made: The buyer should not have made an opening offer without sufficient information, and the shop owner should not have accepted the first offer made. How could the buyer have gathered more information? By using a "hammer," also known as a "push back," a negotiator's objection to a position or request to his counterpart for a concession. Rather than approach the shop owner with a price, the buyer could have said, "The statue is a little weather beaten and has some chips in the surface, and the $199 price is quite steep for my budget. [Here comes the hammer.] What can you do for me on the price?"

This invites the other side to make the opening offer (always to your advantage). What if the owner dropped the price to $150 and said he would apply the 10 percent discount of that weekend's storewide sale to that price? Then the buyer could have reassessed and maybe made another, even lower offer. As it turns out, the statue reminds the store owner of his first wife and he becomes agitated every time he walks past it. He would have given it away for his cost ($50).

Hammers/push backs are variations of "I need more" or "You have got to do better than that" and can be used with great effect. Of course there is a range of intensity and humor with which the hammer/push back can be delivered. For a gentle hammer, you might say, "Can we work on those delivery terms, can you help me there?" or "Can we sharpen the pencil on that price?" More insistent would be "Be reasonable!" or "We're making progress on that issue but the going is slow." More aggressive hammers might be "We're not even in the same solar system, let alone the same galaxy!" or "I didn't just come down the Clyde in a banana peel" (an expression often used by my father—I have no idea what it means, but that has never stopped me from using it to mystify my opponents).

How do you respond when someone uses a hammer on you? Think Elwood P. Doud. Do you remember the dotty but loveable character played by Jimmy Stewart in the movie *Harvey*? Every time someone made a polite general suggestion about getting together ("Let's get together some time"), Elwood P. Doud would turn to them seriously and say, "Well, what did you have in mind?" Use the same comeback if an opponent springs a hammer on you ("You've got to do better than that!"), you sincerely say, "Well, make me an offer," or, with your best Jimmy Stewart voice, "What exactly did you have in mind?"

Negotiating Principle: The Negotiator's Attitude

You don't need a poker face to be an effective negotiator, but it helps if you learn how to strike an "I'm-interested-but-not-desperate attitude." You can imagine how the garden statue scenario above would change if the buyer had gushed to the shop owner about his excitement at finding the exact statue from his childhood he had wanted in his own garden for many years. Do you think there would have been any price concessions made?

There is nothing mandatory about a negotiation. It is entirely voluntary and is driven entirely by the self-interests of the parties. The single largest point of leverage any negotiator has is the willingness to walk away from the bargaining table if acceptable terms are not reached. If a negotiator is not willing to walk away should bargaining pull the deal below his bottom line or is desperate to close the deal, it will be sensed by the opponents, and the price of a settlement will jump higher.

Herb Cohen, a prolific writer and speaker about negotiation topics, teaches that the correct attitude for a negotiator is "I care about making a deal here...but [with a shrug] not T-H-A-T much." If a negotiation does not find an acceptable transaction at the end of the day, the world will not end. The sides will leave the table, and life will go on. T-H-A-T is the attitude to bring to a negotiation.

Of course, it helps if you have an attractive alternative to a negotiated solution. This is a point to be considered when planning a negotiation. Determine your bottom line and be prepared to walk away if the deal is not going to close within your range of acceptability, but also consider your alternatives at that point. When you walk away from the bargaining table, where will you go next? If you are a salesman representing a popular or competitive product, it may not be more complicated than moving on down the line to the next prospective customer. If a serious dispute is being negotiated, the best alternative may be to propose more negotiation sessions, mediation or arbitration, or some other form of dispute resolution. If you don't plan for a fallback position, it may be going to court.

Merit, More Merit, and Principle

It's easy to get disoriented in the give-and-take heat of a negotiation. Remember to evaluate all proposals by their merit. Insisting on a merit-based negotiation forces the other side to justify its numbers and, especially in negotiating a dispute, stops them from throwing out large numbers backed up by nothing but a threat. It is most effective to respond to a sky high opening offer with a simple request that the counterpart breakdown the figures so you can understand where such a high number comes from. I learned this lesson as a young lawyer. In a lawyer's demand letter stating that his client had been injured by our client's negligence and her damages exceeded $450,000, the senior lawyer working with me sent an immediate reply asking for breakdown details and justification for the claimed damages. It bought us time and it surprised the other side, which was not prepared with an immediate answer.

Merit, fairness, justification, value. Every outcome in your negotiations must be perceived as fair and just. If it's not, the negotiation will not succeed. If one side feels the other is not being fair, he or she will simply walk away. I have had great success grounding all negotiation discussion in fairness and insisting that the other side address the merits of their positions. Listen to the merit argument behind this splendid bit of negotiation on the purchase of a refurbished computer from a local electronic store:

> *Customer:* "Hi! I'm looking for a fair price on this used desktop computer."
>
> *Store Salesperson:* "This is a beauty isn't it? The Mach3 2000. When it was new a couple years ago, we sold it for $2,200. It is fully refurbished, and this weekend we are selling it for (looking at the printed price tag) $575. Now *that's* a bargain."
>
> *Customer:* "Why a price of $575? It's a used computer, and with this older operating system, I've seen the Mach3 2000 in other stores right here in town for under $400."
>
> *Store Salesperson:* "I can see you've done your homework! I could go as low as $500. Any lower than that I would need my manager's approval, and he's been in a bad mood all day."
>
> *Customer:* "I appreciate that. It may be a fair price, but I haven't been convinced. Have you seen one of these refurbished models selling for $500 or more anywhere else in town?"

Store Salesperson: "I'm glad you asked. Take a look at this advertisement in today's paper. There's even a picture: a Mach3 2000 for $525."

Customer: "Does it say anything about the operating system?"

Store Salesperson: "Um, yes. It runs Windows XP."

Customer: "And yours runs on an older operating system, Windows ME. Should that lower the price?

Store Salesperson: "Well, yes. Usually by about $50."

Customer: "And what about business software?"

Store Salesperson: "Let's see. The ad says it has MS Office 2003."

Customer: "And yours has Office 1998. How much for an upgrade?"

Store Salesperson: "About $170 if we do the upgrade"

Customer: "OK. So that brings the value of this computer to about $280. Would you say that's a fair price?"

Although insisting on a merit-based exchange may seem like an obvious point, it is important to note how often it helps in a negotiation.

Special Considerations When Negotiating Disputes

Negotiating a dispute sure *feels* different from negotiating the purchase of an automobile or a garden statue. Do usual negotiating principles even apply? It can be tough to work creatively for a win-win solution when the other side is threatening to file a lawsuit or has already filed a lawsuit. Emotions run high, people are defensive, and communication is cramped or nonexistent. The fact is the principles of negotiation apply to dispute resolution with full force. Let's consider how they can be applied.

Responding to Threats of Litigation

> *Look, if we can't work this out, you should know that we have already retained the most aggressive law firm in the state to take you and your organization to court. The damages we seek in a lawsuit will be ten times the proposal on the table now. Take our offer to settle this problem today or the next sound you hear will be the marshall knocking at your door with a summons.*

Ah, the ultimate American power play. How should you respond? Under your cool exterior, your primary goal is to avoid just this result. You want to keep the discussion going and find a way to resolve the dispute before the lawyers come to vacuum your wallet. Here are a couple ideas for responding to a threat of litigation.

> *First of all, Mike, I have never responded well to threats when I am negotiating in good faith. If there are mutually satisfactory grounds to resolve this dispute, let's find them now. We have been working on a resolution off and on for more than four weeks, and I think we are getting close. Drop the threats, please. Filing a lawsuit is the easy part, Mike. Anybody can file a lawsuit. And there will be plenty of time to give wheelbarrows full of money to our lawyers if it comes to that. I think our challenge is to work hard to avoid the expense of a lawsuit. Let's roll up our sleeves and get this done.*

Keeping the Lawyers at Bay: Merit-Based Negotiation

I have found that if lawyers have been hired, they will insist on being included in any discussions about settlement. Often as not, at least one side has a vested financial interest in the terms of settlement. They will often also insist on leading the discussions, effectively setting the tone for the resolution process.

As we learned with the used computer negotiation, merit and principle should anchor the give-and-take, even in a dispute negotiation. If damages are claimed, they should be supported by facts. If attorney's fees are demanded, copies of bills should be produced. If lost wages are being claimed, time records should be evaluated. If a personal injury is at issue, doctors' reports and bills must be produced for review.

If a lawsuit has been filed and includes sky-high claims for damages, start at the bottom and work up, not from the top and work down. Suppose in a personal injury case the lawsuit claims damages of $400,000. The plaintiff in negotiations starts by offering a concession and accepting $350,000 to settle the claim. The defendant wants to start from the other end, building from zero, and see the evidence for the various components of the plaintiff's damages. Damage claim amounts inserted in lawsuits usually have no foundation in facts; they are concocted to put an upper limit on such unknowables as emotional distress. Insist that you see the real information underlying the claims. Ignore the claims, and look for merit.

Tone It Down and Listen

Many people in the midst of a stressful lawsuit get deeply defensive; they go on the attack or simply choose to ignore what is being said by the opponent. Your objective is to get past the lawyers and let the opponent be heard, to let her know that you are empathetic and want to hear about her complaints. The expression of empathy, usually through careful, active listening is one of the keys to conflict resolution. The challenge is to work around or through the lawyers to set up an opportunity to reach this level of communication. Tone down the rhetoric, don't pound the table in anger; ask your lawyer to sit quietly, and invite your counterpart to talk. If the attorney on the other side starts into his case, tell him that you appreciate his perspective on the legal issues, but that you want to hear directly from his client so that you can understand the dispute thoroughly. Assure the room that no statements made in the discussion will be used against anyone's interests. No comment will come back to haunt either side; it is a meeting off the record. You want to listen and understand. You want to mirror the comments to show you understand, and you want to ask open-ended questions in order to encourage the discussion to continue.

As with any negotiation, this careful communication will hold the keys to the ultimate resolution of the dispute. Make notes of particular needs or interests expressed by your opponent so that any mention of motivating facts or circumstances can be recalled clearly after the meeting.

The Last Yard Can Be the Toughest

It happens frequently in dispute resolution: You have agreement on all but one small issue, and on that last issue one side has dug in its heels. It can be a huge psychological barrier and comes to symbolize the entire dispute. I have found that for a relatively small concession, giving in on that last point and closing the deal, you can gain an enormous amount of goodwill. Often as not, it's in your interests to let the other side have the last word.

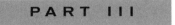

PART III

The Court Avoidance Tools at Your Command

Discourage litigation. Persuade your neighbor to compromise whenever you can. As a peacemaker the lawyer has a superior opportunity of being a good man. There will still be business enough.

—ABRAHAM LINCOLN

ANY EFFECTIVE DEFENSE AGAINST LAWSUITS WILL EMPLOY A FEW VERY powerful tools. First among these is the power of contract. Every businessperson and professional who uses contracts may by a simple addition to those contracts avoid the courthouse entirely for claims and disputes arising under those agreements.

Notices and warnings are everywhere in our lives but some are more effective than others in discouraging lawsuits. They are misunderstood, often misused and underused tools.

One of the fastest growing areas of lawsuit abuse is the employment arena. Savvy employers are adopting dispute resolution systems to side step much of the litigation threat from their employees.

These tools are available to everyone and are discussed in this section. They should be working for your business.

Using the Power of Contract to Stay Out of Court!

For more than half a century, the courts have consistently agreed that parties to a contract can decide the process by which any disputes under the contract are to be resolved.

Contracting for Private Dispute Resolution

Resolving disagreements can be built right into the terms of the agreement at the beginning of the relationship, long before any dispute arises. On the other hand, any contract that is silent on dispute resolution invites the parties to sue one another in court.

It works like a champ. If you place a provision in your contracts that requires the parties to arbitrate any dispute under the contract, there is a

99.5 percent chance that the dispute will never see the inside of a court-room. Federal and state courts have consistently upheld this principle. The public policy of private dispute resolution is most attractive: it alleviates the crush of cases on the public courts docket and shifts the responsibility and expense of disputes from the public to the parties directly involved.

It is also attractive from the perspective of the parties, and it's becoming more so as the courts become more crowded and court rulings less predictable. With agreement on dispute resolution, the parties to a contract can address and eliminate some of the wasteful and time-consuming aspects of litigation: the endless discovery, the preliminary motions, the uncertainties of a jury, the award of punitive damages, the absurd class actions. All of these can be addressed in advance or at the time the parties commence the dispute resolution procedure.

For example, you can decide that discovery will be limited to a single request for documents and interrogatories may be limited to one set of no more than 25 questions. You can determine that damages will be limited to compensatory damages only—with no punitive damages allowed. You can agree that any claims brought under the contract must be made within one year of their occurrence and that the parties agree to waive the right to a jury trial. You can select a mediation/arbitration organization to administer the dispute resolution process and, perhaps most important, when the parties are not in the same city or state, predetermine *where* the process and any hearings take place.

The dispute resolution advantages available through simple contract provisions are truly extraordinary. There is no more powerful tool available for avoiding the courthouse, and it is surprisingly underused by most businesses and professionals.

One reason it is underused is that it carries with it something of a prenuptial syndrome. At the beginning of a contractual relationship, no one is really that interested in dwelling on the terms of any possible divorce. In my view, however, businesses and professionals do themselves a huge disservice by neglecting this powerful legal tool. It need not be negative in tone. There is no reason it cannot be evenhanded and fair. And most people (if not their lawyers) appreciate the gentler approach that will save both sides from the expense and delay of hammer-and-tong litigation.

Arbitration and Mediation

An election under the contract for arbitration will be governed first by the terms of the arbitration language, second by the rules adopted for the arbitration process, and finally by force of the Federal Arbitration Act. There are also state arbitration laws that may apply to enforce the terms of the agreement. If your contract contains an arbitration provision, and the other party files a lawsuit seeking damages, you need only file a motion with the court to "stay" the litigation until an arbitration process can be completed. Except in extraordinary circumstances, such as a demonstration by the other side that the entire contract or the arbitration provision itself became part of the contract by fraudulent means, the court will issue a stay order, stopping the lawsuit in its tracks.

Electing arbitration in your contracts also gives you an opportunity to select an arbitration service provider and a set of rules to govern how the arbitration will be conducted. Of course, you may also devise your own procedures for conducting arbitration, such as predetermining the number of arbitrators to judge the case (usually one or a panel of three), providing the rules of evidence, limitations on awards, and who will bear the costs of the arbitration process. Arbitration is *entirely* a matter of agreement between the parties.

A quiet, hidden advantage of electing arbitration in your contracts is that you can specify *where* that arbitration will take place. That election will consistently be enforced by the service agency you use to administer the proceeding. A national organization with its headquarters in Dallas can specify that all arbitration proceedings must take place in Dallas. There is simply no comparable certainty if matters are left to litigation; often as not the parties will race to their local courthouse to make sure the case is in their own backyard.

Arbitration is the classic alternative to litigation because it has well-settled law enforcing it. Can you elect other types of private dispute resolution, such as negotiation, mediation, or a mini-trial? You certainly can.

They are becoming more and more popular among businesses, but their legal effect is not as well established.

Many of my own clients have found success with a three-tiered provision that first requires the parties to negotiate in good faith. Then, if they cannot resolve the dispute, it will be submitted to nonbinding mediation with a professional mediator acceptable to both sides. If it still cannot be resolved, it will be submitted to binding arbitration with an arbitrator selected mutually by both parties.

Here's what a three-tier provision looks like:

> *Dispute Resolution.* In the event of any dispute, claim, question, or disagreement arising from or relating to this Agreement or the breach thereof, the parties hereto shall use their best efforts to settle the dispute, claim, question, or disagreement. To this effect, they shall consult and negotiate with each other in good faith and, recognizing their mutual interests, attempt to reach a just and equitable solution satisfactory to both parties. If they do not reach such solution within a period of 60 days, then, upon notice by either party to the other, all disputes, claims, questions, or differences the parties agree to try in good faith to settle the dispute by mediation administered by the American Arbitration Association under its Commercial Mediation Rules. If they do not reach resolution in mediation, then, upon notice by either party to the other, all disputes, claims, questions, or differences shall be finally settled by arbitration located in [your city] and administered by the American Arbitration Association in accordance with the provisions of its Commercial Arbitration Rules; provided that this arbitration provision shall not apply on a multiple-party or class-wide basis.

While there have been occasional cases that have enforced a contract provision that mandates mediation for the parties if a dispute arises, it almost doesn't matter whether mediation can be mandated. Negotiation and mediation are important informal preludes to the relatively formal binding arbitration. The language gives the parties time to work it out, and it puts the brakes on the eager lawyer who wants to be the first to file for arbitration to gain a strategic advantage. I like this language because it puts so much distance between my clients and the courthouse.

Look back at the last couple lines of the provision. It specifies that the arbitration may not take place with multiple parties or as a class-wise basis. This language responds to a 2003 Supreme Court ruling that said when an arbitration provision is silent about its application to multiple parties, it is up to arbitrator to decide whether the matter should proceed as a class action. This language gives a clear direction to the arbitrator, and stops this class-action arbitration nonsense cold in its tracks.

Presidents in a Bottle

One Baltimore lawyer is well known for a unique contract provision that offers an unusual insight into the value—and the means—of avoiding litigation. If a dispute arises under the contract, she requires the two presidents of the contracting parties to spend not less than two hours together in a personal face-to-face meeting discussing nothing other than the dispute. After that time together, if the dispute still exists, either party is free to file a court action.

Not only does this provision immediately stop the early and mindless shovel pass to the lawyers, but it keeps the parties-in-interest involved in the decision making as long as possible. And what president is going to have the patience and passion to discuss a dispute for two hours with another businessperson and not find mutually acceptable grounds for settlement?

She hasn't seen her clients in court yet.

Using the Power of Notice
In-Your-Face Fine Print

THOUSANDS OF CASES HAVE IMPOSED LIABILITY ON PROPERTY OWNERS, MAN-ufacturers, and professionals for failure to advise people in advance of risks inherent in a product's use or an activity or service, even if those risks are obvious to everyone old enough to eat solid food. The rush of lawsuit liability has certainly had its impact on our society. You can't turn around without being warned that prescriptions drugs may have stomach-turning side effects, that riding a roller coaster is physically stressful and may cause a heart attack, or that the proprietor assumes no responsibility whatsoever for the safety of your possessions. The more idiotic the lawsuit that found liability for failure to warn, the more foolish and insulting will be the notice that business subsequently posts to customers and clients:

- A high school student tries out for the school's cheerleading squad, and when not selected, she appeals to a court of law. In the future, a puzzling legal statement accompanies the competition announcement: "Decisions of the cheerleading judges are final."
- A car rental company renting a car in Tampa to be dropped off in Miami is held liable for millions in damages when two renters take the car to a dangerous neighborhood in Miami to ask directions and are robbed and injured. The theory? The rental company failed to warn them about that particular high crime area near Miami. Read the fine print notices in Florida next time you rent a car there.
- In 1996, a Tucson resident sprained her ankle when she stepped in a gopher hole while in a public park. In 2001, a jury awarded her an eye-popping $450,000. According to the plaintiff's attorney, "The case hinged on the city's responsibility to post adequate warnings about burrowing animals and to provide a safe alternative to dodging holes and caved-in tunnels." Can you imagine the outdoor signs that when up in 2002?
- The packaging of a fishing lure with three curved steel hooks warns: "Harmful if swallowed."
- Bicycle shin guards warn their users: "Shin pads cannot protect any part of the body they do not cover."
- A baby stroller label cautions parents (who must not be paying attention): "Remove child before folding."
- A bottle of drain cleaner displays this charming bit of lawyering (this stuff can't be taught in law school): "If you do not understand,

---

Warning notices follow a philosophy worthy of H.L. Menchen:
When posting a warning notice no one
has ever incurred liability by insulting
the intelligence of the
American public.

---

or cannot read, all directions, cautions, and warnings, do not use this product."

Some of these absurd warnings, and many others are gathered by the M-Law organization in Michigan (www.mlaw.org).

What Works?

Businesses and professionals need to re-evaluate the basic warnings, notices, and cautions that they provide their customers and clients. All too often, those statements are written by lawyers with no sense of the impact (if any) the communication has on the reader, and their clients follow their advice as if there is some sort of mojo magic conveyed by the mysterious legal words. Notices and warning are often poorly understood by the businesses that use them, so they are hidden away on poorly photocopied, wholly unreadable forms. They are so common that no one actually reads the caution language; they just sign where they are told. Low-level business administrators and front desk workers know they have to get a signature, and they don't think beyond the signature on the form.

Let me summarize the thinking and recommendations I make to clients about warnings, notices, and cautions:

- *Use plain English!* Legalese simply does not convey meaning to the average non-lawyer reader. Do not write your notice for the judge who hears the case where the warning label is introduced as evidence. Write it for the product user or the client in the first instance. Make sure the notice can be easily understood by the user/client. The sign posted on the business premises need not convey all possible details and limitations in a wall of impenetrable fine print. Deliver the headlines, and point to the immediate availability of more detailed information elsewhere: a pamphlet available on request, a Web site page, and online video clip, a CD mailed to you on request.
- *Put risks in perspective.* Risk is part of life. There is no need to scare the reader by listing every risk that sports an infinitesimal chance of

occurrence. Don't be afraid to share your experience, carefully based on facts.

- *Be positive and confident* (never arrogant or unfeeling) in tone.
- *Convey that you are human*; humans make mistakes.
- *Make a clear statement of accountability.* You are responsible for the things you can control, and have taken every precaution to deliver the highest quality product/service possible. There are many things you cannot control, such as the customer/client role in giving you information about their needs, frailties, and weaknesses. Convey that you are a responsible member of the community who takes pride in delivering the best of products/services. You want to hear from the customer immediately if there is a problem or question about your product or service. Provide contact information if someone does have a problem or question.
- *Take the opportunity to improve your customer/client relationships.* Because this is a perfect opportunity for an intimate dialog with your customer, so write any cautions or notices with that in mind: reach out, thank them for choosing you or your product, deliver a clear message, and invite responses and comments.
- *Be creative!* Use available media, your web site, or your preservice meetings. If you are a physician, consider an interactive video program to educate your patients while they sit in your waiting room. While waiting in the privacy of an inner room (in that breezy robe), the patient could select information at the push of a button about his or her particular area of complaint. Risk warnings, cautions, and limitations can be naturally folded into this information presentation.

If you do find yourself hauled into court as a defendant in a civil tort case with the plaintiff asserting an extreme theory of liability based on lack of notice, it will be most valuable to your legal position—if you simply cannot avoid the courthouse—to have delivered a warning notice that the plaintiff actually read (or viewed) and could understand, rather than a dense set of legalese form statements that flashed by for a quick signature and then were gone.

If a plaintiff says she had no opportunity to read the fine print, was simply told to "sign here and here," did not receive a copy of the statement she signed, and was not really warned about any of the risks she was taking, you can imagine how fast a court would throw it out.

Indeed, a clearly stated, easily understood warning notice about some of the risks of your product or service will go a long way to helping you stay away from the courthouse. At least it will discourage those cases where the plaintiff's theory is that you failed your duty to advise of a particular risk associated with your product or service.

Cleaning House

Can you anticipate in advance what aspect of your business or service is vulnerable to attack based on a failure to notify of a danger? In many cases, you can. Start with your records of reported injuries, misuse of the product, or complaints about the product or delivery of the service. It is natural that your pride in your products will lead you to be dismissive of complaints or reports of problems, but step back for an objective review. What do you find? Note any recurring problems, patterns of concern expressed by your own personnel, or past legal problems.

You are primarily looking for any problems or dangers that your organization has identified and may have decided did not warrant action. It is *prior knowledge* of a defect or dangerous condition that will hang a company in front of a jury. Remember the McDonald's hot coffee case from Arizona? An 81-year-old woman bought a 49 cent cup of coffee at a drive-through window of a McDonald's restaurant, and when she tried to remove the plastic top to add cream and sugar, the coffee spilled into her lap, causing second and third degree burns in her groin area. She sued and was awarded $2.9 million, later reduced on appeal.

When the hot coffee case hit the headlines, it caused a sensation and became fodder for howling late night comedians and sober editorial writers across the country. It's easy to see that case, at least in headline form, as the ultimate idiot's notice case. Everyone knows coffee is served hot. What part of "hot" did this woman not understand when she bought the hot coffee? The jackpot award made it appear that the courts had finally entered a looking glass world of absurdity that was truly unbeliev-able. The evidence that sunk McDonald's was not the fact that the spilled coffee was particularly hot (20 degrees hotter than any other cup of cof-fee served in the Phoenix market by other vendors), or that the customer was partially responsible for the accident (in its calculations the jury reported that they scaled back their award figure by 20 percent on the theory that the customer was partially responsible for the spill). What sunk McDonald's was that the company had received numerous reports of scalding, had even settled some lawsuits for coffee scalding, was well aware of the dangers of coffee served at higher than usual temperatures, and had taken no action, showing, to the jury at least, a rather callous disregard for potential customer injury. Juries hate even a whiff of cor-porate callousness.

What could the company have done? Suppose it had evaluated the dangers posed, produced a management report, put in place a responsive program to lower the serving temperature or give customers a choice of temperatures, and issued a clear notice to customers about the potential dangers of spilled coffee. It might have headed off the courtroom train wreck before it started.

Some cases seem absurd in their outcome when viewed in isolation but are in fact the culmination of a series of corporate miscalculations and inattention to developing problems in the business or the professional practice.

The Key

The key to avoiding lawsuits? Five words: *build a culture of accountability.* A well-written notice of potential danger is perched on the tip of an ice-berg; accountability is the body of the iceberg itself. It gives weight and meaning to the notice; it is the real protection behind any consumer/client notice. The McDonald's cup carried a small announcement that the contents were hot, but it was hardly effective in overcoming the compa-ny's real corporate failing, its fundamental lack of accountability on a serious problem.

The best notices not only achieve the effect of warning customers, clients, or patients, but they also convey the basic accountability of the company or professional behind the notice. Most warning signs and printed notices achieve exactly the opposite effect; they shout about the things for which the company is NOT responsible. This is a significant lost opportunity for most organizations and is often an ineffective approach to avoiding court. Figure 10.1 illustrates some examples.

FIGURE 10.1: Better Notices

Traditional Negative Notices	Stronger Statements
"We are not responsible for valuables left in your car while parked in this garage."	"We are careful in our operation of the XYZ Garage, and we're proud of our award-winning safety record. But protecting your valuables and other items left in your car is outside of our control, so we cannot be responsible for them. Please do not leave valuable items in your car. Take them with you. And please remember to lock your car while you're away. We'll be here when you get back. Thanks for using XYZ Garage!"
"Use the park at your own risk."	"Welcome to Sheppard Street Park. We hope you enjoy your visit and that this visit to the park is a safe one. As with all outdoor recreational activity, there are some risks inherent in the activity. Your use of the park is at your own risk, and we hope you exercise appropriate caution."

FIGURE 10.1: Better Notices, continued

Traditional Negative Notices	Stronger Statements
"Do not feed the animals."	Welcome to the Anytown Zoo. Your visit to the zoo should be enjoyable for you and our animals. They are on carefully controlled, special diets to maintain their health. Please do not offer them any food or drink, or throw food or drink of any kind into their enclosures. This is a serious offense in our zoo, and if we see any food being offered to our beautiful animals, we will ask you to leave the Anytown Zoo immediately.

I think you see the point. Notices can convey pride and accountability. They can be positive statements of your limits as an organization; they can welcome your customer. They don't have to snarl and bark to be effective, and they need not be weighed down with legalese. Notices need to communicate clearly; if a significant number of your customers speak a language other than English, consider printing a parallel notice in their language. The goal, remember, is to avoid court. The notice should be targeted to your concerns and limitations of your product or service and well positioned so that it is easily seen and understood by all of your customers. Just imagine how the warnings and notices will be presented by a plaintiff in a lawsuit:

- "I never saw any sign."
- "Sure, I signed three or four pieces of paper with tiny writing on them, but I never had a chance to read them. Besides, I hate reading fine print."
- "It's all legal gobbledygook to me. That notice was nonsense. I couldn't make any sense out of it!"

A well-written and clearly presented notice will speak for itself; and it will speak volumes about your organization.

As we discuss in Chapter 19, accountability takes on several functions in avoiding a court of law.

Controlling Employment Disputes with Internal Corporate Programs

E MPLOYERS HAVE HAD A PARTICULARLY DIFFICULT TIME MANAGING THE FLOOD of lawsuits by employees against their employers. The popularity of corporate conflict resolution programs is a healthy and necessary response. They are designed to identify and resolve all disputes in the workplace at an early stage, before a conflict can ripen into a serious problem that ends up in court.

Taking It In-House
In-house conflict resolution programs come in all shapes and sizes. They take the form of an ombudsperson or ombuds program, a mentor program, an outside mediation service, or a peer counselor. They involve var-

ious degrees of training, orientation, practice, and if done well, will have the support and involvement of senior management.

Conflict resolution programs can be mandatory or voluntary, although even a "mandatory" program will leave room for employee choices. An employee can sidestep a mandatory program in a number of ways: avoiding an issue completely, putting things off for later when it will most likely be harder to resolve, challenging the program in court, withholding his or her productivity, or electing to use more traditional alternative dispute resolution (ADR) tools.

The ultimate goal of all dispute resolution programs—the definition of success—is widespread employee support and participation. If employees stay away in droves, it doesn't matter how the program is structured or how effective it may be at resolving problems. The challenge is to build employee acceptance, to change choices they make, and to encourage tackling a conflict at the earliest stage possible.

It can be a mistake to exclude management from the program or limit the types of disputes that can be presented to the resolution process. An in-house dispute resolution program can be an important step in transforming your organization's culture, top to bottom. That won't happen if it doesn't have the full involvement and the unflagging support of top management, or if it has a limited, confusing approach to the type of disputes that can be handled. It will take a sustained effort over time on several fronts to establish the idea in the minds of employees.

Set Up

To get off on the right foot, consider asking for employee input into the formation and structure of a dispute resolution program. Convene a representative committee of employees to examine options and best practices and to report back to the president. What will fit best with the company's culture? What structure will be most responsive to employee needs? How can it assure confidentiality and a complete absence of company red tape? What type of training will be necessary at the beginning and on an ongoing basis? What expenses will be incurred and what budget figure is appropriate?

Who You Gonna Call? The Ombuds Model

An ombudsperson possesses a degree of independence in the organization, and is appointed to listen confidentially to employee problems, to facilitate and mediate, to resolve, and to help employees find the best resolution possible. He or she usually reports directly to the president or the vice president of administration, and is therefore independent of department or division bias. The model of dispute resolution, as adopted by a large manufacturer client in the Midwest, breaks down into these steps:

Step 1

The ombuds listens, discusses options, and offers advice. It is all confidential. He or she will contact the parties involved to present issues and seek an informal solution, perhaps conducting a mediation conference. The ombuds will draw factual conclusions and make final recommendations to the parties.

Step 2

If not resolved by the ombuds alone, he or she will create an ombuds team, a panel that is comprised of the ombuds and a peer of the person who initiated the complaint. The team will then examine the situation and provide a new set of recommendations for a solution.

Step 3

If still not resolved, the matter may be submitted to binding arbitration, depending on the particular requirements of the person's employment agreement.

This model can be changed and tailored, of course, to the particular needs of each organization. However it is structured, the basic thrust of these programs is the same. The ombuds is an approachable listener who is not a threatening manager up the chain of command, but rather someone who offers a side door entrance to top administration managers. In order to assure the success of the Ombuds Model, the ombuds must be:

- Independent within the structure of the organization,

- Fully supported by senior managment, and
- Trustworthy.

There is no question that internal dispute resolution programs make a giant step toward a culture of accountability, and they are important investments for keeping an employer out of court.

CHAPTER

Controlling the Escalating Dispute

DISPUTES TEND TO ESCALATE. THEY SEEM TO TAKE ON A LIFE OF THEIR OWN, generate their own momentum and their own internal logic. The arrival of lawyers on the scene and how you handle that event can determine whether or not this dispute is headed for court.

Every business owner and professional needs to be an effective conflict manager, and the first step in that direction is learning the fundamental structure of all conflicts.

Anatomy of a Conflict

All conflicts go through a generally predictable evolution as they slump their way toward resolution. In my experience, there are six stages of a conflict:

Stage 1: Combat

This is a time of emotional chaos. It is the fog of war, a time of dizzying action, but most of all it is a time of uncertainty. Think back to how you felt in the few days following the attacks on September 11, 2001. In the heat of combat, the future is unknown and seems to be thrown into great doubt. Combatants are off-balance, and fear can quickly set in.

You are confronted with someone spewing cuss words at you and threatening reprisals, or you perceive a disturbing threat that has not yet completely emerged. A driver, claiming you were involved in a hit-and-run accident, accosts you in a parking lot. You receive a formal letter from an attorney demanding money for his client's damages and threatening legal action. At the office a supervisor accosts you and demands that you cooperate with him or he will "make your life miserable." A policeman comes to the door of your home saying the neighbors have been complaining about noise at your property late at night.

We come to grips with the idea, a disturbing idea for most of us, that we have developed an enemy.

The conflict at this stage has no shape or form. Emotions (anger, resentment, pride, disappointment) run high. There is no resolution in sight. It is not linear in any sense. And there is no process in place for addressing the swirl of concerns caused by the conflict.

Stage 2: Containment

In this stage, you take preliminary steps to put your arms around the conflict. You take a step back from the immediate threat and assess the situation. Thinking beyond the conflict is a form of containment; a lawsuit is a rough form of containment. A response that offers to hold a meeting has the effect of containing the conflict. A process emerges. The disputants relax a bit and consider the implications of the conflict.

Stage 3: Confrontation

This is the pivotal point in any conflict, and an essential part of conflict resolution. We do not mean that there is a confrontation in the threatening sense of the word. The essence of this confrontation stage is to simply address the conflict, the facts, and feelings involved, in a mature, calm manner. A face to face meeting to discuss concerns is the type of confrontation that wil address this important stage of a dispute (and may, if handled well, keep you out of court).

Stage 4: Compassion

This most human of emotional responses is an essential element in finding a constructive resolution of any conflict. Compassion is the key to strengthening the underlying relationship. The most common expression of compassion in our dealings with others is *listening*. Not just *hearing*, but actively, intently listening with a single-minded focus on the speaker.

Stage 5: Negotiation

This is a process by which the negotiating parties work to find grounds of mutual benefit; through creativity you work to expand available benefits. The same dynamic is present when negotiating resolution of a conflict: the parties work to address interests and resolve the dispute based on their real needs.

Stage 6: Resolution

Once the terms of resolution are decided, it is always advisable to put them down in writing. This allows the parties to create a clear path and clear goals to meet in the future, although even if the terms are not memorialized in writing, the resolution stage resolves the conflict.

"Blimey, Cap'n, They're Flying the Jolly Roger!"

Escalation occurs in the initial *Combat* stage of a conflict. The initial dispute is not addressed immediately, for whatever reason (but it's usually a combination of pride and fear). We know what happens next; it jumps to a higher level. Unless handled, it will jump to a higher level again. The secret to controlling the escalation is to use techniques that will move the conflict through the stages of the process discussed earlier. Your first task is *Containment*: to define and circumscribe the dispute, to move it out of its Combat footing and give the participants enough perspective on the situation to see beyond the immediate threat of the battle, and then to move the process along to the *Confrontation* and *Compassion* stages.

The great peacemakers of the 19th and 20th century startled the world with their ability to swiftly resolve a conflict by moving from the Combat stage to Containment, then Confrontation and Compassion. President Abraham Lincoln comes immediately to mind, managing the Combat phase of the Civil War with dogged perseverance and then moving immediately to offer terms of surrender to General Lee's army with magnanimity and compassion. The very terms of the conclusion of Combat accelerated a great part of the way through to Resolution.

President Harry Truman expressed his country's Compassion in the adoption of the Marshall Plan for rebuilding Europe after World War II. Even President Nixon and his Secretary of State Henry Kissinger pushed quickly through the stages of conflict resolution in Paris meetings with the North Vietnamese to end the Vietnam War (once the shape of the negotiating table was argued at great length).

Containing Your Escalating Conflicts

We have discussed the idea of an intervention to break the stranglehold that lawyers have on a conflict. When a dispute is escalating, at the first sign that a dispute is stepping up to a serious level, at the first sign of a lawyer's letterhead, at the first sign that you are losing control, consider an aggressive intervention by the people who own the problem—the principals themselves.

In some circumstances, you will want the assistance of a neutral professional to bring the disputants together and conduct a productive face-to-face discussion about the dispute and the steps necessary to resolve it. In most circumstances, it can be handled by the disputants themselves. It just takes initiative.

Many of my clients hesitate on this approach. The other side stormed out of the last meeting vowing to file a lawsuit, or my client received a threatening letter with extreme demands that are wholly unrealistic. "How can we possibly talk now? I don't even want to be in the same room with that jackass. Why should I bother?" It's easier to let the lawyer make the approach, but that may be a huge mistake. This client simply is slipping out of accountability and would like someone else to own the problem. If the lawyer does make the approach in most situations like this, it will simply push the other side to bring in its own lawyer. My rule is always put off attorney involvement as long as possible. Keep the principals working on the problem until they find a resolution.

This is particularly important if the other side is part of a business or professional relationship that may have value in the future. In this case, there is every reason for the principals to get together to resolve the dispute. The approach should always appeal to fairness and perhaps remind the other side about earlier times when their relationship worked well. If at all possible, it should be face-to-face.

If you have received a threatening letter from an attorney, think carefully before you give the entire matter over to your own attorney. It will be hard to get it back. Consider this response (Figure 12.1) to the threatening attorney's letter. Notice it is not written to the attorney.

FIGURE 12.1: Letter to Respond to Threatened Litigation

From the President/Vice President of XYZ Corporation

Dear ____:

We have received your attorney's letter regarding _____. We would like to offer you some background information about XYZ Corporation and explain how we prefer to handle legal complaints that are generated out of our business. We also wish to propose a course of conduct for both of us.

I can personally confirm that XYZ Corporation is fully accountable and responsible for its business activities. We take great pride in our company, and an important aspect of that pride is the serious approach we take to our responsibilities

FIGURE 12.1: Letter to Respond to Threatened Litigation, continued

to our customers, business colleagues, and communities. If our organization makes a mistake or commits an oversight, we are fully prepared to be account-able for those actions. We are people, too, and we understand that people are not infallible.

We have pledged as a company to explore and participate in all available forms of alternate dispute resolution prior to filing a legal action in a court of law. We have found that we can resolve our differences more quickly and to the satisfaction of all parties with a healthy attempt to allow the principals to fashion their own solutions through negotiation or mediation, or some other form of creative problem solving.

We believe that our courts should be used as a forum to resolve civil disputes only as a last resort, after all other efforts to resolve our difficulties have failed to bring disputants to a resolution. We see this conservative use of our courthouse resources as a responsibility of all citizens, so that our courts are not burdened with unnecessary case filings.

As of matter of corporate policy, we are committed to make all reasonable efforts to resolve our disputes directly, maturely, and fairly. This makes good business sense. We often learn ways we can improve our business, and the exchange of views affords us an opportunity to build better relationships with people who may have a complaint about us.

At the same time, this company has a low level of tolerance for abuse of our public judicial systems. We object strenuously to so-called junk lawsuits and other baseless forms of corporate harassment.

We do not respond well to threats. For instance, we do not respond to threats to sue us in court if we do this or don't do that. We do not respond to demands for payment or action with a time limit or deadline that threatens a subsequent court filing. While we believe that access to our judicial system is a right of all Americans, we refuse to be threatened with being named as a defendant.

We are not at all afraid to engage in the judicial system; indeed, we have on retainer a retinue of fine attorneys who are quite eager to protect our interests in any courtroom in the land. Rather, we have found that with a measure of cre-

FIGURE 12.1: Letter to Respond to Threatened Litigation, continued

ativity and goodwill we can fashion better solutions than the courts when we take responsibility for those solutions ourselves.

We are committed to understanding your concerns and complaints about our company and exploring fair terms of addressing those concerns. In our experience, we will have more flexibility in finding solutions, and frankly, more sympathy with our conflict partners if we can explore these concerns *before* a lawsuit is filed.

Many lawyers prefer first to file a lawsuit so that they can gain leverage in discussing "settlement" even before the other side has an opportunity to address the underlying concerns of the situation. We understand this somewhat traditional approach, and we think it is a particularly thoughtless and expensive form of coercion in 2005. Let me assure you that our evaluation of the merits of your complaints will not change if a lawsuit has been filed. What will change is our level of enthusiasm for listening to your concerns as well as the range of options for solutions available to us.

We suggest that you and we plan as soon as possible for a face-to-face meeting with a senior decision maker in our organization to discuss your concerns. We may be able to find an acceptable solution at this meeting; I certainly hope so. We may decide jointly on a second meeting or a course of mediation so that we have the assistance of a resolution professional or other resolution assistance. We will discuss next steps at our meeting.

Should your attorney and one of our attorneys attend this meeting? We will leave that up to you. If you would be more comfortable and you think it would be productive to have your attorney at the meeting, then feel free to include him or her. We will not have any attorney in this meeting unless you decide to include your counsel; and we will not meet with your attorney without your attendance. Legal squabbling at this information meeting would be counterproductive, and we urge you to discuss this with your counsel so that it is clear this is a business meeting looking for creative solutions, with supportive counsel invited to assist in helping all of us understand the facts and fashion possible solutions.

You will not be pressured to make any decisions at our meeting, and you will have every opportunity to consult with your legal counsel. We will consider the

FIGURE 12.1: Letter to Respond to Threatened Litigation, continued

meeting to be "for the purposes of settlement only" and "off the record," and "without prejudice" to any claims that anyone may have. No statements made in our meeting should come back to haunt any of us. It is truly an opportunity for you and us to understand one another's concerns and, if appropriate, to look for constructive solutions together.

By the way, if your attorney wishes to write again, please have him direct his correspondence to our legal counsel, J. P. Winterbottom, IV at [firm name, address, telephone number]. Mr. Winterbottom will advise me on any legal issues that pertain to our consideration of the situation, but I will remain responsible for addressing your concerns and, I hope, resolving them.

Please contact me/my assistant at [telephone number] so that we may make arrangements for a meeting. We look forward to the opportunity to explore your concerns in person.

Very truly yours,

XYZ Corporation

By: Vicki Vice President
cc. [Attorneys for both sides]

Not only is the response not written to the threatening attorney, it largely pushes the threatening counsel aside to deliver its important messages to the principal. It is written by an executive of the company, not its attorney. It expresses accountability and a genuine intent to work in good faith to resolve the dispute.

Toward Resolution Out of Court

Your responsive letter sets a constructive tone for the meeting, and the complaining person arrives with an attorney in tow. You and your attorney plan to attend.

Your role at this meeting is twofold. You want to underscore the accountability of your organization and your willingness to explore her concerns, and second, you will listen, question, and listen more. You express compassion by listening intently. This is the heart of the reason for this first meeting.

Be prepared to propose next steps—mediation, another meeting, an evaluation and exchange of information by the lawyers, a mini-trial, or formal arbitration. If threats of litigation are made in this meeting, have a ready response about alternative ways to resolve a serious dispute.

> *"Look Beth," making your comments directly to the principal, not the attorney, "we have made good progress today. We are not on the same page yet but I think we are getting there. If we end up giving this matter over to our lawyers, I will see that as a failure of reasonable people to communicate well and find creative solutions to their problems. Besides, if you pursue this in court, as I said in my letter, it cuts down our options for finding solutions that make sense to us both. Your lawyers and our lawyers make money and we will be back here in a few months or years with the same problem on the table. Let's redouble our efforts before it gets to court. How about another meeting next week?"*

Your meeting has moved you through the confrontation and compassion stages of this conflict, and it has teed up the next negotiation step. You asked questions, listened intently and took notes, all with an eye to gathering the information you will need to find a negotiated solution. Do not shy away from asking questions about personal circumstances and personal interests. Ask 'ultimate objectives' and press for what the principal thinks is 'fair.' Don't ask her lawyer these questions, it will only draw a recitation of the inflated claims to be pursued in court. Most lawyers will jump in on these questions nevertheless, not wanting their client to understate or undercut her claims. Remind everyone in the meeting that there is no posturing necessary, the meeting is completely off the record, and no comments will come back to hurt anyone's legal position.

Armed with a wide ranging discussion of personal circumstances and interests, you have already made progress in the negotiation. Apply your negotiation skills from Chapter 8.

The next meeting will advance the negotiation and with a little luck you can bring both sides to the point of resolution.

This negotiation process takes the disputants through the steps of conflict resolution and if aggressively and carefully applied will increase your odds of staying out of court.

Sometimes You've Got to Fight the Bully

One attorney friend of mine thought about the subject of my book a few seconds, and he put it succinctly with a twinkle in his eye, "The only way to stay out of court is to be lucky enough to avoid the asshole lawyers in your life." In my office, this has become known as the Sibel Solution, for its author. Some business people and their lawyers use the courts for their own purposes, and they have found success in suing their partners, vendors, employees, and contract counterparts. The legal process is used in a totally unscrupulous way by these characters, and they tend to find their own definition of success. If you find yourself going up against the unprincipled lawyers and their lawsuit-happy clients, there is little that can be done to avoid the courthouse. No amount of intervention or appealing to fairness will turn them away. Of course, when used as a sword, the abusive legal process is designed to make the other side capitulate rather than spend ungodly sums chasing a principle like fairness or truth. In these legal battles, locating and identifying the truth—the real truth—is a luxury that will come at an unbelievable price, and even then it may not be the basis of a ruling by a judge or jury. Sometimes you simply have no choice but to fight the bully or to give in to his demands, surrender, and cut your losses.

PART IV

Alternate Dispute Resolution (ADR) Tools

If appeasing our enemies is not the answer, neither is hating them. . . .
Somewhere between the extremes of appeasement and hate there
is a place for courage and strength to express themselves in
magnanimity and charity, and this is the place we must find."
—A. WHITNEY GRISWOLD

WITH THE GOAL OF AVOIDING COURT BY THE APPLICATION OF SKILLS, tools, and attitude, to this point we have looked at the conflict resolution and communications skills you need to stay out of court! The tools you will need to apply to the task are grouped under the rubric alternate dispute resolution, or ADR. We will touch on the major ADR techniques in the pages that follow; but it

is not by any means an exhaustive treatment of the subject.

Mediation

The Greatest Dispute Resolution Tool Ever Invented

MEDIATION IS AS OLD AS DISPUTES AMONG PEOPLE. IT IS A DISPUTE RESO-lution technique in which a neutral third party meets with the disputing parties and helps them find their own resolution to the problem. Mediation is not binding; it is entirely voluntary. I think of it as "professionally assisted negotiation," and in the hands of a good mediator, the process is remarkably effective.

To be a true believer in mediation, you almost have to see it work. Imagine two neighbors who can barely speak to one another after years of fighting between their families over everything conceivable: noise late at night, property lines, landscaping, spite fences, trash in the yard, and on and on. They come together in a room with one or two mediators and work through their dispute. Each side is heard fully by the mediators, and then they are invited to sit in separate rooms while the mediators meet and speak confidentially with each side. Issues are listed and possible solutions explored. They all come together again, and the mediators review the situation, revealing, to the surprise of the disputants, that they have been listening very closely. They identify the issues to be resolved and the creative ideas that have been suggested to address each of the issues. They set a positive atmosphere that relaxes the disputing sides and efficiently work through all the issues, one by one. At the end of the afternoon, they reduce the agreed upon course of conduct to writing, an informal contract, and the two sides shake hands, smile, and sign the agreement.

When you see two sides heading into the mediation room without a prayer that they can resolve their differences, and then see them walk out with a resolution in hand, you realize the power of mediation. It works so well for several reasons. The fact that it is nonbinding says to parties that they have nothing to lose. They can sit through the mediation and walk away at the end of the day no worse off than when they began. So there is little resistance to the process. It also gives people a chance to be heard and a chance to say things to the face of their counterpart that they need to get off their chests. In conflict resolution, there is nothing quite as valuable as the opportunity to let off steam and air a complaint. That is also the motivation of a lot of litigation, and it disappoints litigants when they realize that the actual trial and steam letting are years away, and in all likelihood won't happen at all. During a mediation hearing, the mediators, if not both sides, listen closely to what is said. They can keep the speakers on track. And they can draw responses from the other side so that issues are illuminated.

Mediation is also efficient and inexpensive. A half day or full day's hearing can be planned for the cost of the meeting room, if any, and the mediator's fee. It can be set up so that lawyers are involved in the hearing, or not, and mediation has no time-consuming rules imposed on the process.

Many mediators invite parties represented by legal counsel to prepare a very brief (three to five page) summary of the legal issues and background considerations to be submitted a few days prior to the hearing so that the mediator has an overview of the dispute before the hearing begins.

Most court systems now require litigants to go through mediation before they may proceed with their court claims. This succeeds in eliminating many cases and alleviating the courts' crowded dockets.

The Mediation Process and What You Can Expect

As with most of life's endeavors, you will get out of mediation what you put into it. At a law conference a while back, I was told by a plaintiff's litigator—maybe he was just strutting his hardened litigator image in front of other lawyers—that the courts in his state require mediation, but he never expects a favorable outcome and puts zero effort into mediation hearings. "It's a waste of time. I just sit there for the session because the rules require it, and then we can get on to court." Among traditional lawyers, litigation is high test, bitter, and strong caffeinated coffee. It's the real stuff, a manly brew. Mediation is decaffeinated tea, hardly worth the effort.

That lawyer was not seeking the resolution of a genuine dispute; he was after the payoff down the golden road of the lawsuit. I wondered how his client felt about that attitude, although he was most likely on a contingency fee, so the client could care less about actually resolving the dispute. They wanted to roll the dice in front of a jury. That's where the big jackpots happen—either in front of a jury or by way of a hefty settlement payment by an exasperated defendant.

Not all mediation sessions will be rewarding, especially if court ordered. I have had better experience where the parties themselves and their lawyers want to resolve a genuine dispute and then get on with their lives. There are a number of organizations that will provide mediation services. The American Arbitration Association (www.adr.org) is the oldest and probably best known. I am only slightly biased given my association with the AAA as a member of its National Panel of Neutrals. When the parties contact the AAA seeking mediation, they will pay a case set-up fee, and the mediation will be conducted in accordance with the Mediation Procedures published for the particular category of dispute (commercial, construction industry, or employment). AAA provides a procedure by which a mediator is selected and also makes available a conference room in one of its centers if the parties agree on that location. The parties generally split the costs of the mediation equally: set-up fees, room charges, and the mediator's published fees.

The mediator conducts the hearing and does his best to move the parties toward a settlement. If successful, a settlement agreement will be drawn up by the mediator or the lawyers representing the parties, and just that fast, the dispute will be settled. If not successful, the parties should discuss whether it would be productive to schedule another mediation session, submit the dispute to binding arbitration, or to apply another ADR tool.

Avoiding Court

Mediation is an indispensable tool for avoiding lawsuits. It may be proposed at any time in the life of a dispute, even after a lawsuit has been filed. It is a useful intervention tool once attorneys get hold of a dispute because it gets the principals in the same room without the chilling interference of the lawyers.

Mediation also functions to move a dispute past the Combat phase through all successive stages to Resolution. The opponents have the chance to contain the dispute, confront the issues (face-to-face), express compassion (by listening and responding carefully), and negotiate a resolution.

If there is a challenge to mediation, it is the fact that it is voluntary and takes a large measure of good faith by parties to tackle a genuine dispute, as opposed to a lawsuit for profit. The skill level of the mediator plays a large role in the success of the mediation process. Really good mediators are difficult to locate and hard to identify from the list of possible mediators provided by the AAA or another mediation service provider. Look for people who have had solid training in mediation and several years of experience. Ask around for recommendations.

If you manage a business or practice one of the professions, you should line up a mediation process with a highly skilled mediator well before you need the service. Build it into your contracts and your communications with vendors, employees, and clients. Make convenient and nonthreatening dispute resolution part of the service you provide. If a dispute breaks out, you do not want to waste time looking up mediation service providers in the Yellow Pages. This is the first tool in your lawsuit avoidance tool kit. Keep it sharpened and near the top of the kit box for quick use.

Arbitration

A RBITRATION IS WHAT MOST PEOPLE THINK OF AS THE ALTERNATIVE TO LITI-gation IN a court of law. It is a process by which a dispute is submitted to a single impartial arbitrator or a panel of three arbitrators, and the arbitrator(s) makes a final and binding determination (the "award"). An arbitrator decides the case presented in essentially the same manner as a judge, he, she, or they will hold an evidentiary hearing, review the evidence and testimony presented at the hearing, and then issue an award. The award is final, binding on the parties, and enforceable in a court of law.

Arbitration is entirely a creature of contract. It takes place only when the disputants agree on submitting their dispute to arbitration. It exists because the parties have agreed on it, and it is entirely governed in substance and procedure on the agreement of the parties.

Compared to litigation, arbitration has a number of strengths and advantages:

- *Written agreement.* A written agreement to use arbitration can be inserted in all contracts, at the time of a dispute or well in advance of any dispute, and it will be enforced in any court by preemptive federal law and numerous state laws. The contract provision can also address the particulars of the arbitration process, the rules that will apply, and the limitations to be placed on the arbitrator—all in specific detail if that's what the parties want to do.
- *Privacy.* Arbitration hearings are closed, and the proceedings are not a matter of public record.
- *Simple rules and informal procedures.* There is no formal discovery in an arbitration procedure, but the arbitrator may direct the parties to exchange key documents. The strict rules of evidence do not apply, and there is no requirement that a transcript be produced of the testimony offered or the arguments made. The rules adopted to govern the arbitration, such as the Commercial Rules of the American Arbitration Association, can be changed by the agreement of the parties.
- *Experts as arbitrators.* The parties can choose an effective arbitrator based on his or her expertise in the subject matter of the dispute. There is no need to educate a judge about the subtleties of your business or profession.
- *Money saving.* Arbitration is generally less expensive than litigation, largely because there is no extensive discovery or discovery disputes, no extensive and time-consuming preliminary motions, and no appeals of the ruling.
- *Speed to resolution.* Statistically the great majority of arbitration cases are concluded within 12 months of filing.
- *Narrow grounds for appeal.* Courts will enforce an award of an arbitrator and will generally review the arbitration only if there were substantial defects in the arbitration procedure. They do not review the substance of the case or the application of the law to the facts in the case.

Weighing the Choice: Litigation or Arbitration?

Even with these clear advantages over most litigation cases, arbitration is probably not the best forum for all cases, and there is considerable debate among lawyers as to the relative merits of arbitration and litigation. Plaintiff's lawyers will gripe about the expenses associated with arbitration (the case administrative fees, having to pay the hourly or daily rates of the arbitrator(s)), and attack as myth each of the economic and speed of resolution advantages noted above. They argue that the very absence of rules makes the process slow, contentious, and difficult in the absence of a judge's authority and experience.

The arbitration process can certainly be abused by relentlessly aggressive or manipulative legal counsel, and the otherwise simple, quick decision-making process can bog down into an elongated series of hearings without the civilizing procedural rules of a courtroom. Even if some of this criticism is true, arbitration will for most cases be a better choice than litigation. Sure, some lawyers and some arbitrators can wreak havoc in an arbitration setting, just as the same lawyers can abuse lawsuit procedures. But the arbitration process, especially if preceded by mediation, offers disputants their best chance at a quick and fair resolution. There are no juries to contend with (no juries inflamed by plaintiff's counsel to "send a message" by hammering the defendant with huge damages), and with some effort at the beginning of the case, you can find an unbiased, solid citizen who understands your business to hear the case and make a fair award.

In a sense, arbitration offers disputants the same sort of dispute resolution that was offered by the American court system 60 years ago, before the procedural abuses of the late 20th century set in. Discovery is abbreviated, the process is run by common sense rules of testimony and evidence, hearings are brief and to the point, awards are decided promptly, and appeals are few and far between. What's not to like?

Variations on the Arbitration Theme

- *Mandatory court arbitration.* Many courts have adopted a mandatory arbitration system by which claims that fall under a certain amount, exclusive of attorneys' fees and costs of $50,000 or

$100,000, are submitted by the court to arbitration with an attorney randomly assigned to the case to sit as arbitrator. The arbitrator issues an award; if one of the parties does not accept the award, he may file a new case in court. If both parties accept the award, however, it becomes binding.

- *High-low arbitration.* This damage control procedure will be helpful where there is no issue regarding liability, such as a personal injury suit, but the dispute is about the amount of damages. Claimants tend to exaggerate their claims in court or arbitration, just as defendants tend to understate the damages suffered by the claimant. In high-low arbitration the parties agree in advance to the parameters of the award issued by the arbitrator; the claimant agrees to a maximum award in exchange for the defendant's agreement to a minimum award floor regardless of the amount of the award by the arbitrator.

- *Baseball arbitration.* Again, this method can be useful if the parties agree that some amount of money will be paid by one side to the other. The approach was developed by professional baseball teams in settling salary disputes. After the arbitrator holds a hearing, each side recommends to the arbitrator a figure it proposes to settle the matter, and under the rules of baseball arbitration, the arbitrator may select only one of the two proposed figures. This dynamic forces both sides to moderate extreme positions out of concern that the arbitrator will find the other side's figure more reasonable.

Class Action by Arbitration

One area of fast moving change, and increasing abuse by the sue-for-profit industry, is the class action. Plaintiffs' lawyers, no doubt frustrated by the effectiveness of arbitration provisions keeping plaintiff customers out of court, have sought to conduct class action arbitrations based on an arbitration provision in a consumer contract. The U.S. Supreme Court ruled on such a claim in *Green Tree Financial Corp. v. Bazzle*, 123 S.Ct. 2402 (2003). The plaintiffs sought to pursue a class-wide claim under an arbitration provision that was silent on whether such a class-wide claim was permissible. Green Tree Financial, now known as Conseco Financial Corp., argued that it should be allowed to handle the claims individually under its arbitration provision. The South Carolina Supreme Court had ruled that the claimants could proceed on a class action basis in the arbitration, and the arbitrator issued an award of $27 million to a class of 3,374 homeowners. On appeal, the U.S. Supreme Court ruled that where an arbitration provision was silent regarding the availability of class actions, the arbitrator, and not a court, must decide whether a class action was permissible. The case was sent back to the arbitrator to decide the question of arbitrability.

This sent hundreds of companies and their defense lawyers scurrying to add to their arbitration provisions an additional sentence that says something like, "This provision shall not be apply to multiple parties and shall not apply a class-wide basis."

If you want to stay out of court by using an arbitration provision, make sure it is clear on this point of class actions.

Mini Trials and Other Creative Techniques

W HEN YOU ARE ACCOUNTABLE FOR YOUR BUSINESS OR YOUR PROFESSIONAL life, you *own* disputes as they arise. You do not shovel them off to someone else (including your lawyers until it becomes necessary), and you do not expend your energies lining up your excuses for the situation. You take control of the situation and seek to apply your own personality, skills, style, and creativity to the problem. Never be discouraged from a creative solution if you think it will make progress toward a fair resolution.

The Mini Trial Is Not a Real Trial at All

The mini-trial concept has two meanings. It can be used to describe an abbreviated formal process where the essence of a case is presented before a magistrate or a judge, and a non-binding ruling is issued. The ruling is designed to help the parties advance in their settlement discussions by giving them an idea of the results they can expect if they proceed with a full case presentation.

Another application of the same basic idea is even more innovative. Imagine that for two years the Ajax Grommet Company has been disputing the contractual responsibility for a shipment of allegedly defective grommets sent to the World Wide Engine Company. Settlements talks have stalled, and Ajax lawyers are about to file a lawsuit to try to collect the $450,000 owed for the shipment. World Wide suggests a mini trial where each side can present the essence of its case in front of two senior officers, one from each company. Each officer has the authority to settle the dispute. Also sitting with the officers is a neutral facilitator whose job it is to make sure the presentations by the lawyer adhere to the essential facts and move along within agreed upon time limitations. At the end of the presentation, the facilitator makes a written recommendation to the officers, who then meet in private to discuss the case and, if possible, bring the settlement to a successful conclusion. In some reported examples of mini trials, disputes that have taken years of effort to resolve have been settled in a few hours by executives whose eyes have been opened to the strengths of the other side's case.

Legal observers commonly comment that when discussing their cases with their own clients, lawyers tend to emphasize the strengths of their own case and diminish the strengths of the other side's legal position. Executives who are shown in mini trial what a case would look like in court receive a clear, unvarnished look at both sides of the entire case and can use that information to find, sometimes quickly, the best possible settlement.

The mini trial is especially useful in disputes where a large amount of information needs to be exchanged and/or presented in order to assist in the settlement process. Either type of mini trial can be expensive, of course, given the legal efforts involved. Although this procedure is also not right for every dispute, the mini trial illustrates a creative, private, and tailored dispute resolution process that can be used to keep a dispute from bogging down in a court of law.

There *are* alternatives to spending years grinding through fortunes in legal fees and wasted time, crossing legal swords that ultimately have nothing to do with real issues of importance to the parties involved.

Creative Solutions

Several years ago, Herb Kelleher, the legendary CEO and a founder of Southwest Airlines, resolved a dispute over trademark rights to an advertising slogan in characteristic flamboyant manner. He challenged the president of the other company to an arm wrestling match rather than leave it to the lawyers to spend hundreds of thousands of dollars in a drawn-out legal battle. The two presidents arm wrestled for the rights to the slogan, winner take all. The match was held with a flourish of valuable publicity, and the dispute was decided in minutes with two out of three pins.

More recently, in 2003, a £70,000 dispute between two New Zealand telecommunications companies over access to a mobile radio network was settled in the same way. The bested chief executive told ABC News Online, "Sure, losing hurts but not nearly as much as paying lawyers' bills."

Not all CEOs would be interested in an arm wrestling match to resolve their companies' disputes, but the point is a valuable one. Our arm-wrestling presidents realized the limitations of traditional dispute resolution methods, and showed confidence, accountability, a sense of fun, and a touch of chutzpah. They refused to shuffle the dispute to their disinterested lawyers. They continued to own it themselves and took the initiative in its resolution.

ADR Organizations That Can Help

A CONTRACT PROVISION THAT CONFIRMS THE PARTIES' AGREEMENT TO USE arbitration to resolve disputes will also usually designate a professional arbitration service provider to handle the administrative process of the arbitration. These ADR organizations provide an invaluable service. They help the parties select a city and place for the proceeding (you can select the location in your contract); they select the arbitrator and preserve his or her neutrality in the case; they oversee procedural questions, and they move the process along so that it does not become bogged down in animosity.

The Granddaddy AAA

The American Arbitration Association was formed in the 1920s shortly after the adoption of the Federal Arbitration Act. It is a nonprofit organization and probably the best-known arbitration/mediation organization in the world. The AAA focuses on handling business disputes and has issued rules and procedures for three categories of disputes: commercial, employment, and construction. The AAA handles more than 250,000 disputes each year and has a roster of neutral mediators and arbitrators numbering more than 8,000 worldwide.

The association has developed an efficient means of case administration. When a case is submitted to the AAA, it is assigned to a case administrator, a staff person (usually a nonlawyer) who is responsible for moving the case along, managing any objections or questions about the arbitrability of the case, receiving any counterclaims from the respondent, securing the appointment of an arbitrator who has no conflicts of interest and is acceptable to both parties, and scheduling a preliminary hearing (if one is needed) and an evidentiary hearing. Each stage is set for completion with deadlines met by the case administrator. Within 48 hours of the case assignment, the administrator contacts the parties by telephone, usually in a conference call. An answer is requested within 15 days of the initial contact, and hearings are scheduled to make sure they can be attended by the parties and their legal counsel. Within 30 days of the hearing's conclusion, the administrator transmits the award from the arbitrator to the parties, and it is done.

Under the AAA rules, the parties do not communicate directly with the arbitrator, except at scheduled hearings, but instead deal directly with the case administrator. This preserves the neutrality of the arbitrator as a decision maker and allows a professional staff member, not the neutral arbitrator, to keep the process moving.

Don't be misled by the name. The AAA also provides mediation services. The mediation management process is roughly the same. If you and your disputing counterpart decide that the assistance of a mediator might help resolve the matter, you simply contact a local office of the AAA and request submission of the new matter for mediation. A case administrator is assigned to the case, the parties select a mediator from a list provided by the case administrator, and a mediation session is scheduled.

For a list of regional and local AAA offices, go online and click on the AAA web site at www.adr.org.

CPR Institute for Dispute Resolution

CPR (formerly the Center for Public Resources) is a dispute resolution organization that was formed in 1979 and provides both arbitration and mediation services. It is a nonprofit cooperative effort among corporations, law firms, and academic ADR specialists offering a self-administered dispute resolution process, which means that the arbitrator is directly involved in the administration of the case. Further, the parties are free to work with CPR in the selection of the arbitrator or they may bypass CPR altogether and pick the arbitrator themselves from CPR's list of available neutrals.

The CPR process provides a procedure by which an arbitrator's award may be appealed. The grounds of appeal are that the award contains one or more material and prejudicial errors of law, or the award is based on factual findings not clearly supported by the record. Of course, it also accepts the grounds set forth in the Federal Arbitration Act for vacating an award. Appeals are heard by a panel of experienced arbitrators who are former federal judges sitting as "appellate arbitrators." For more information, see www.cpradr.org.

JAMS/Endispute

The Judicial Arbitration and Mediation Services (JAMS) is the largest of the private, for-profit organizations providing mediation and arbitration services. The ranks of their arbitrators are made up almost entirely of retired federal and state judges, with some attorneys selected for their experience and expertise. JAMS also provides an optional process for appealing an award before a panel of arbitrators. For more information, see www.jamsadr.com.

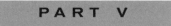

PART V

The Mindset Key

Establishing an
Ethic of Accountability

It is easy to dodge our responsibilities, but we cannot dodge
the consequences of dodging our responsibilities.
—SIR JOSIAH STAMP

S O FAR, WE HAVE DISCUSSED TWO IMPORTANT LEGS OF THE STAY OUT
of court stool: conflict management skills (such as negotiation)
and tools (such as contract provisions and notices). The third leg of
the stool, building an ethic of accountability, is an attitude, a state
of mind, a corporate culture. It is at once the most important of the

three and the hardest to master and put into effect. The first step in

building an ethic of accountability is to banish the victim's mindset

from your organization.

The Victim's Mindset and Other Enemies of Dispute Resolution

A S NOTED IN CHAPTER 3, YOU CAN SPOT THE VICTIM'S MINDSET. IT HAPPENS to everyone at one time or another (no one is immune), and sadly it is a consistent outlook on life for many. There is no other aspect of dispute management that has as subtle and debilitating an effect on our efforts at conflict resolution.

If you are defensive, pointing fingers, angry, indecisive, willing to wait to see if it works itself out, and unwilling to roll up your sleeves to discuss a problem, or if your organization and its culture do not encourage and support accountability, you will have an impossible time resolving disputes early, when money and energies can be preserved. Take a look at the list of comments in Figure 17.1. You may recognize yourself or your company. Which side do you fall on?

FIGURE 17.1: Comments

The Victim Mind Set and Other Enemies of Dispute Resolution	We Are Accountable: Helping Dispute Resolution
"It's in the hands of the lawyers now. There's nothing I can do."	"What else can we do to bring this dispute to resolution?"
"Let the lawyers talk to those s.o.b.s. I won't waste my time."	"I'll call the principal on the other side again myself."
"No comment."	"If anyone in my company made a mistake, I want to apologize. We are responsible corporate citizens and accountable for our good works— and our mistakes."
"It's not my job to solve these problems."	"Have we explored all negotiation alternatives? Can we redouble our efforts here?"
"Jason messed up this situation long before I got here last year. It's entirely his fault. Why should I even get involved?"	"This dispute is tying up five of my key people. Let's resolve it now."
"See you in court."	"See you at our mediation session."
"We have to send a message."	"We have to get on with business."
"Let's wait to see if they have the money to litigate this case for any significant time. I happen to know they don't have much money."	"As a company, we have pledged to explore all alternative dispute resolution techniques before we file suit."
"He's a jerk. Ignore his demands, and I guarantee he will go away."	"We don't let things slide here. A complaint comes in, we evaluate it and respond."
SNAFU (Situation Normal: All Fouled Up, or words to that effect.)	ADR PDQ (Alternate Dispute Resolution Pretty Damn Quick)

FIGURE 17.1: Comments, continued

The Victim Mind Set and Other Enemies of Dispute Resolution	We Are Accountable: Helping Dispute Resolution
"The guys upstairs really screwed it up this time."	"Let's take the lead and roll up our sleeves."
"It's really the design team's fault we're in this mess. Let *them* fix it."	"There is no 'we' and 'they' in this organization. It's all WE!"

Evaluation of statements such as these will give you a quick insight into the culture of the organization involved. Are people willing to pull together and bring an optimistic, self-confidence to the company's affairs? Does everyone recognize that they are on a team with a clear goal? Are they committed to that goal? Are the principles of accountability clearly stated in the company's materials, and are they reinforced by top management? Is there a can-do attitude that accepts responsibility and is willing to take the lead?

Victims will ignore a worsening conflict situation, hoping it works itself out or goes away. They will give it to the lawyers and hope they never have to think about it again. They are not committed to victory in the sense that resolving the dispute is the objective. Fear has crept into their thinking, and they exhibit neither confidence nor perspective on the situation. Other emotions (anger, bitterness, embarrassment, a passion for revenge) are almost always involved. The victim mindset drives people to take the emotionally easy way out, and it explains a lot of the finger pointing and whining.

These absences of manifest accountability are deadly in resolving disputes. They exacerbate conflict, and I think they are among the leading reasons that so many lawsuits are filed. A mistake is made, and the subsequent complaint is completely ignored or rejected out of hand (hoping that the complainer will be discouraged and just go away). Then someone files a lawsuit purely as an attention-getter. The lawsuit has become a tool to force the organization, professional, or individual to listen and take someone seriously.

The victim's mindset is raised to a high art form in court and is used effectively by lawyers representing the parties in a dispute long before the dispute actually gets to court. The victim's position appears in virtually every demand letter written by his or her attorneys. My client has been victimized and injured, it asserts, and you are directly responsible for his damages, pain, and suffering. Most legal disputes are little more than formal attempts to identify one party as the victim and the other as the victimizer.

Compare that thinking to the mindset of accountability. An accountable person is a realist; she sees her problems as her own and does not blame others for what is essentially her responsibility. The accountable person is willing to discuss a conflict and solve it. If a mistake is made, the accountable person takes responsibility for the mistake and does not pass the buck. This makes an enormous difference in conflict resolution.

"It's Not the Money"

What is it that every personal injury plaintiff says is the motivation for a lawsuit? "It's not the money, I just want the company to be accountable for their conduct. I don't want this to happen to anyone else." (Of course, Caffey's First Rule of Transparent Quotes states that if any plaintiff or his lawyer says it's not about the money, it's about the money.) It has become a cliché in post-case comments (usually after a whopping award for the plaintiff) that the plaintiff says, "The entire lawsuit could have been avoided if only the defendant had apologized." Now, this may or may not be true, but there is nothing that inflames the motivation of potential litigants like being ignored or arrogantly rebuffed by an organization or professional that won't listen to them or take them seriously. That's one reason that doctors and hospitals have reduced the number of malpractice lawsuits by apologizing to the patients if a mistake is made. Psychologically, this shows a very human (and vulnerable) face to the patient and makes it more difficult to pursue a lawsuit.

Apology Construction: "Well, excuuuuuse me!!!!"

Not all apologies are alike. In a dispute that may have legal consequences, it is important to convey an apology without accepting liability for the situation, especially before all the facts are determined. Take a look at Figure 17.2, which is a series of apologies, both good and bad. Those on the left convey causation neutral apologies without crossing the line:

FIGURE 17.2: Good and Bad Comments

Causation Neutral Apology	Taking Too Much Responsibility Before the Facts Are In
"We're terribly sorry for your son's condition."	"I can't tell you how sorry I am that my mistake caused your son's difficulties."
"I'm so sorry for your additional discomfort in recovery."	"I'm sorry. My scalpel must have nicked your sciatic nerve, causing your leg to go numb."
"I'm terribly sorry about your difficulties during the operation."	"I apologize for my team leaving behind a sponge in the incision."
"On behalf of the entire surgical team at Memorial Hospital, I am sorry for your experience and your pain."	"I'm truly sorry that I failed you. This certainly was not my best work."
"I'm sorry you had so much bleeding during surgery."	"I'm sorry I nicked the artery and caused so much bleeding."
"We are sorry for your injuries from the wall collapse. We know you broke your leg when it came down, and it must be so painful."	"We apologize for the wall collapse; we must have used the wrong cement mixture."
"We're sorry about the discomfort you experienced after using our product."	"We feel terrible that our product gave you the hives."

Figure 17.2: Good and Bad Comments, continued

Causation Neutral Apology	Taking Too Much Responsibility Before the Facts Are In
"For the entire company we want you to know we are sorry for your broken leg, and we understand from your letter that you lay blame for your injury on one of our products. We will be looking into that point of fact. We would also be very concerned if there is any defect in the design of our CrutchSupport system."	"We feel just terrible that our crutch bolt gave way and you broke your other leg."

These are extreme examples chosen to illustrate a few important points. The goal of an apology in the face of a dispute is to convey the empathy we all naturally feel, and to express accountability, rather than stating that your actions caused the results that evoke your sympathy and thus are legally liable for the situation. You can acknowledge a person's suffering, loss, discomfort, difficulty, or damages WITHOUT admitting or assuming causation between your actions or products and the other person's injury or problem, at least until all the facts are in. The key concept and the legal danger in an apology is *causation*. Many people in our society are naturally inclined to express empathy and personal guilt (whether or not justified) by assuming that somehow they are fully responsible for a damaged person's situation. So many people in a stressful situation will also continue talking from nervous energy and do not stop when the point is made and it's time to stop talking. Issuing an apology in a legally sensitive situation takes care, some training, and considerable control.

The award for the Most Legally Pristine Apology of the new century has to go to NBA basketball star Kobe Bryant, issued as prosecutors were about to drop criminal charges against him. According to reports in the

Washington Post and elsewhere, Bryant's accuser insisted that he issue an apology before the rape charges would be dropped. His lawyers must have worked into the night crafting the required statement. It is an apology only a lawyer could love and is completely devoid of any causal link. Here, in part, is what he was scripted to say:

> *I want to apologize to her for my behavior that night and for the consequences she has suffered in the past year. Although I truly believe this encounter between us was consensual, I recognize now that she did not and does not view this incident the same way I did. After months of reviewing discovery, listening to her attorney and even her testimony in person, I now understand how she feels that she did not consent to this encounter.*

Bryant accomplished what he and his legal team set out to do. He expressed empathy by acknowledging his accuser's feelings and the "consequences she has suffered," but did not assume a direct causation (or any causation) between his behavior and responsibility or liability for (her perception of) his behavior or its consequences. His apology was a weak expression of accountability, but a masterful piece of legal work.

An effective apology should be:

- *Empathetic.* It should express the speaker's *feelings* and address and acknowledge the personal *experience* and *feelings* of the victim. This is not the time to review facts or discuss what happened.
- *Causation neutral.* It must not assume that the speaker's actions were the cause of the victim's experience, at least before all the facts are in.
- *Excuse free.* Resist any urge you may have to cite excuses for your actions.
- *Genuine and sincere in tone.* A remarkable professor of mine, the late Earl Latham of Amherst College, used to say to his students, "Sincerity, you know, is one of the more cosmetic virtues." If your apology is not expressed from genuine feelings of empathy and

compassion or if it is insincerely expressed, you will hurt more than help your position. Remember that one of the pillars of conflict resolution is the genuine expression of compassion.

- *Brief and to the point.* This is not the time to ramble on about the situation. Make your point, express your feelings, and then stop talking. Naturally empathetic, talkative people have a tendency to accept more guilt and responsibility than is called for by the situation.
- *Based on listening.* Use your active listening skills. The person complaining often has a strong need to unload his or her feelings or express frustration. It is time for you to patiently listen and acknowledge feelings.
- *An expression of accountability.* I firmly believe that a professional or corporation should always be prepared to articulate its accountability and responsibility for its actions, NOT as an admission of liability or even responsibility for a given situation, but as a matter of general corporate or personal principle.

In my experience, a well-crafted and heartfelt apology should be part of every professional's anti-litigation skills and should become part of the accountability profile of all companies.

18

Preparing the Way Out

STEP BACK FOR A MINUTE AND REVIEW THE EIGHT STEPS AVAILABLE FOR preparing to reduce the likelihood of litigation in your professional or business life.

1. Audit Your Organization's Vulnerability to Lawsuits.

Conduct an audit of your business with an eye toward the areas that need to be fortified against possible lawsuits. Review the outline in Chapter 19 which explains this unusual auditing procedure.

2. Recognize the Victim Dynamic.

Understanding and recognizing the victim dynamic in your own organization is the first step. Your goal is to eliminate the victim dynamic in yourself and in your company. Model accountability by your leadership wherever you can, and train your organization to own a dispute, face reality, and constantly ask the question: *What else can I do to resolve this dispute?*

3. Put a Dispute Resolution Plan in Place.

Be sure to get feedback and input from your organization. You will want the entire organization to buy in to the internal program you adopt. Also take steps to plan how you will respond to outside disputes, especially serious disputes that may threaten to ripen into litigation. Meet with legal counsel you know and trust will fit well with your dispute resolution style, and discuss your theories. Locate and interview mediators so that you know who you can call if you need mediation assistance. Having a complete plan in place will give confidence to your entire organization; it will show your support for an aggressive, accountable approach to conflict resolution.

4. Put a Public Relations Plan in Place.

For businesses and professionals, a dispute that finds its way into the media will call for a very public response, often under intense pressure. Yours is a position of accountability and responsibility. You and your organization are important members of the community, and you must not let a lawsuit make you appear to be anything less. Consider the public relations aspects of a public dispute, and plan who will speak for the company and the roles to be played by your lawyers, your public relations firm, and your senior managers. If the company is sued for sexual harassment or some other noxious behavior and a senior human resources executive (not the one designated to handle the public statements for the company) is ambushed in the parking lot by a television crew, what should she say when asked about the lawsuit? An embarrassed "no comment" and a hurried dash to her car may not be the image you want shown on the evening news. Discuss in advance how to handle such an "interview," and brief the management team on effective press relations.

5. Own the Dispute.

Show your organization that the entire company owns its disputes. They are not mistakes or anomalies, but a part of business life that must be acknowledged, seriously embraced, and promptly resolved. Remind your team that there is an opportunity for the company to improve its relationships with vendors, clients, customers, and patients by resolving conflicts in a manner that demonstrates the organization's character and commitment to principle.

6. Know When to Intervene.

Lawyers and business executives unskilled in dispute resolution can place a mutual stranglehold on a dispute so that all involved lose sight of efforts to resolve it and move on. This situation often calls for senior level intervention: arrange a meeting of the principals for a serious discussion of the dispute by those who own it, not just the hired-gun lawyers. Establish an outside resolution advocate, a role unique to American legal practice as far as I know, who will have responsibility for managing the early and efficient resolution of conflicts. (See www.resolution advocates.com.) An intervention may take the form of a settlement conference, a mediation session, or a mini trial. It may simply be a meeting of principals to discuss whether any sort of ADR might be employed to address the dispute and keep it out of court.

Plan to intervene whenever:

- You sense that your team has not recognized a growing dispute on the horizon.
- You see lawyers for another company or person surface in a situation, and they threaten larger problems or make serious demands on you or the company.
- You sense that a dispute in the hands of your lawyers is generating more heat (in legal fees) than light (in progress toward resolution).
- You hear an employee of yours respond to a press inquiry with a "No comment."

- You sense that a meeting between principals, or the involvement of more senior management, will lead to a resolution of the problem.
- You sense that your management team has not expressed accountability or seems not to be making a relentless, sustained effort to find a resolution.

7. Commit to Use ADR Where You Can.

There are a dozen different ADR techniques that might be used to address and resolve a dispute, all of them preferable to going into court and thus subjecting the dispute to the lawyers. As an organization, consider pledging to explore the use of ADR before filing either a lawsuit or counterclaim to a lawsuit.

8. Build Accountability.

Consider seminar training for your executives to foster accountability in the organization. Also consider adopting a statement of accountability that can be adapted by your organization to set the appropriate tone. (See Chapter 19 for an example.) This approach reflects a fundamental belief in the duties of citizenship for the organization. Any culture of accountability is built on such principles as responsible citizenship, accountability for mistakes, and a healthy approach to dispute resolution. It is every bit as important as a company's mission statement.

19

Other Corporate Tools for Accountability in Dispute Resolution

L ARGER ORGANIZATIONS MAY NEED TO APPLY DIFFERENT TECHNIQUES TO ACCOM-
plish the cultural shift represented by accountability in all dealings. We suggest to our clients three tools that have proven effective: a dispute management audit, key questions for discussion by the company's board of directors, and adopting a public statement of accountability.

Dispute Management Audit

A dispute management audit is an evaluation conducted by an outside organization to identify the areas where an organization's approach to dispute avoidance and resolution is weak or vulnerable. An audit might address the areas of corporate management suggested in Figure 19.1.

FIGURE 19.1: Dispute Management Audit

- Review all contracts regarding dispute resolution provisions. Recommend language addressing creative dispute resolution.

- Evaluate any areas in the company where there are repetitive disputes or other conflict problems.

- Review all internal procedures and evaluate how they are working.

- Prepare information about third parties who are available to assist in dispute resolution.

- Institute a process for reporting disputes to senior management before they become serious and threaten litigation.

- Institute a resolution advocate who has authority to intervene early. The role is that of an internal troubleshooter and an external representative to third parties.

- Identify decision makers in the organization who have authority to settle disputes with other organizations.

- Evaluate overall litigation experience and history.

- Evaluate the level of ADR training among the legal department and management teams.

- Evaluate a corporate ethic of accountability.

- Evaluate consumer complaint handling mechanisms.

- Set benchmarks for performance and improvement in the area of dispute management. Evaluate best practices among competition.

Let the audit serve as the first step toward controlling the company's legal costs.

Involve the Board of Directors

Senior management can only benefit from the involvement of the board of directors in setting the tone and policies regarding dispute resolution and litigation. Consider the questions and points of discussion for an upcoming board agenda outlined in Figure 19.2.

FIGURE 19.2: Ten Questions for the Board of Directors

Ten Questions the Board of Directors Should Discuss with Management About Litigation Strategy and Dispute Resolution

1. What is the process in the Company's management by which we decide to file a law suit or respond to a Complaint filed against the Company? Has an emergency response management committee been formed?

2. What general liability insurance does the Company carry, and what claims are covered and excluded? Does the Company also carry directors and officers liability coverage?

3. How do the Company's contracts (employment agreements, licenses, sales agreements, etc.) address dispute resolution?

4. Who is the Company's outside legal counsel? What does he or she advise about the law firm's strategy of handling legal disputes? And does the outside counsel have ADR experience?

5. What portion of last year's legal or other expenses was directly related to resolving disputes?

6. What has been the Company's experience with ADR? What resources (a good mediator, an arbitration program) are immediately available for the Company's use?

7. Is this Company perceived as a responsible citizen in its community, fully responsible for its actions? Does the Company promote an internal culture of accountability, and is the accountability projected externally?

FIGURE 19.2: Ten Questions for the Board of Directors, continued

8. What is the level of training among Company managers in dispute resolution and litigation avoidance?

9. What mechanisms are in place for handling internal disputes?

10. What lessons has management learned from direct experience with litigation?

A Statement of Accountability

The tools we describe above are internal controls, and that is the place to start. But what about the company's external image? Consider the leadership possibilities, both internal and external, represented by a formally adopted corporate statement of accountability. There is no better way to set a tone for company culture than a statement from the very top of the organization. Figure 19.3 is a sample.

FIGURE 19.3: Statement of Accountability

This organization strives to be a good corporate citizen in our community. We shall be responsible for our honest business activity and accountable for any mistakes we might make through oversight or inadvertence or otherwise.

We acknowledge that responsible citizenship includes a good faith effort to resolve disputes that may arise in our business, and it includes using the public courts system sparingly. We are committed to using direct communication and, where appropriate and agreed on, mediation or other appropriate forms of alternate dispute resolution before we initiate litigation in a court of law.

[Signed by the Chairman of the Board and the President]

In our seminars, we provide such a sample statement of accountability on a quick reference pocket card. Can your organization make this statement? This would be a powerful statement to attach to a response to a demand letter from an attorney, or long before it comes to that, attached to a response from the company regarding a complaint from another party claiming injury.

Litigation Means Never Having to Say You're Sorry

There is a grand experiment under way in the medical profession, and it is shaking up the traditional approach to handling physician mistakes, problems in the hospital, and threats of litigation. The hospital and/or the doctors involved disclose information about the procedure and *apologize for their mistakes* and for the discomfort or difficulties they may have caused. Of course, this has traditionally been discouraged by lawyers out of fear that the apology would appear to be an admission of liability. Yield to the very real human urge to apologize, the thinking went, and the other side will use it as a club in the courtroom. The traditional thinking extended this to any comments about the incident by the doctors and the hospital; traditional litigation concerns dictated that the doctors speak to absolutely no one, especially the press, about the incident until it is resolved. Thus, "No comment."

For the past few years, some of the most prominent hospitals in the nation have encouraged their physicians to admit their mistakes and apologize. The results have been more than encouraging. In 2004 the managing attorney for claims and litigation at Johns Hopkins University Hospital in Baltimore was quoted in the *Wall Street Journal* as saying that the hospital's new openness "has helped reduce expense payments related to legal claims by 30 percent in 2003." Studies conducted have shown people to be 1.5 times more likely to sue if the doctor does not disclose the mistake and apologize.

The psychological impact of an apology is perhaps obvious. As one potential plaintiff said, "They honored me as a human being." He refused to sue, accepting in settlement an amount lower than he would have received if he had sued. A doctor's apology for a mistake can deflate the wrath of a medical malpractice dispute. If there is no arrogant doctor denying that he or she made a mistake, there is no anger to inspire in a jury, no conflicting story to spin out in court, no revenge motive inspired in many patients, and no horrified indignation to relate to the court. The victim is much less a victim when the victimizer does not play out his role; instead the injured person was merely hurt by the mistake of a well-intentioned doctor.

This is still tricky ground for doctors and hospitals. As discussed in Chapter 17, there are apologies, and then there are apologies. Apologies certainly do not always deter someone from suing, and there are certainly right ways and wrong ways to apologize for a mistake. The right way is to keep the apology on the human level, a pure empathetic response. It should be neutral on the fault or no-fault of the doctor; the doctor must be careful not to accept too much responsibility for a medical tragedy if one occurred. For instance, the doctor is better off apologizing for the result of a mistake, not the detail of the mistake itself. "I'm deeply sorry that the medication I administered made you so uncomfortable," rather than "I'm sorry that I gave you the wrong anesthesia." In most cases, all the facts are not in when the doctor approaches the patient with an apology, so he or she should not make any assumptions about fault or liability.

Colorado and Oregon have led the nation in adopting legislation that prevents a doctor's apology from being used against him in a court. The "I'm Sorry" laws have been well received by the medical profession, and other states are considering similar measures.

Hospitals have also taken the opportunity to openly discuss problems in a way that conveys its accountability without in any way damaging its legal position at all.

Transcript of Attack Interview in the Parking Lot of the Community Hospital Medical Center

> *Reporter:* "Dr. Jones? Brayden Downing from Channel 27 News. Can I have a word with you for our viewers?"

[Cameraman moves into position. A microphone is thrust in Dr. Jones' face.]

Dr. Jones: "Good evening, Brayden. I recognize you from the television news. How can I help you?"

[Note here: Dr. Jones is not threatened by the approach; he's relaxed and confident. He flatters the reporter by recognizing him, and then calls him by his first name, rather than Mr. Downing. This instantly puts the doctor in a friendly, helpful footing, rather than an adversarial one.]

Reporter: "Dr. Jones, the family of Bobby Dogsbody is outraged that you and your hospital misdiagnosed Bobby's kidney problems, and now he is lying in critical condition in your hospital. They have already met with lawyers who are talking about a multi-million dollar lawsuit against you, your nursing staff, and the hospital. Do you have any comment?"

[Note here: It would be easy to say "No comment," wouldn't it? But Jones steps up to handle the question.]

Dr. Jones: "Brayden, I'm pleased to have an opportunity to address your questions. On behalf of the entire staff at Community Hospital, let me say my heart goes out to the family of any child who is ill, and we certainly all wish this young man a speedy recovery. You have me at a disadvantage this evening because I would like to talk about this situation. But we sincerely respect our patient's privacy and his family's privacy, and I'm afraid that concern must come first. As you and your viewers may know, last year Community Hospital adopted a comprehensive set of patient's rights, and first among those rights is privacy."

Reporter: "Maybe, Dr. Jones, but why not set a higher priority on quality medical care?"

[Note here: The reporter is doing his best to draw an angry reaction from Dr. Jones, a little flash of temper for the six o'clock broadcast would be a hit. Does Jones rise to the bait?]

Dr. Jones: "I think Community Hospital delivers the finest medical care in the state. It is a privilege to work with the dedicated people at Community Hospital, and I am proud to lead the internal medicine team. This is an institution that prides itself on being a good member of our community, and we consider ourselves fully accountable for the medicine we practice. If there are any complaints about our medical care or our other services, we will address them promptly and responsibly, and take appropriate action."

Reporter: "Thank you Dr. Jones. This is Brayden Downing for Channel 27 News. Out."

I provide this dialogue to illustrate a point. There are many things to say instead of "No comment" without commenting directly on the subject matter of the potential lawsuit. Any inquiry from the press gives you an opportunity to talk about what a fine organization you work for, its pride and accountability to the community, even if you do not feel comfortable answering the particular question put to you. It sends a strong message to the community, and it shows real leadership to the team within your organization. It shows you to be confident of your position, secure in your accountability, and proud of the work being done at the hospital. Every "No comment" is an opportunity lost.

Putting the Tools to Work

I can hear what many readers are thinking: Am I opening my company to greater exposure by these approaches? Do we just become a bigger target? If I were to drive home one fundamental point with this book, it is that all businesses and professionals have become targets—BIG targets—and it is time to take steps to counter the wave of litigation sweeping over us. Businesses and professionals have to become smarter and more aggressive about how they handle complaints, how they respond to disputes, and how they respond to threats of litigation. Do nothing and you *will* become a bigger target; it is only a matter of time.

The impact of the new openness in some corners of the medical profession should not be lost on the rest of us. An organization that is committed to full accountability will certainly apologize for its mistakes. It will face reality, come to grips with its implications, and deal with all people in a forthright manner.

These tools should be put in place as soon as possible. They take training and time and commitment to principle. Start this week. Assign responsibility for creating the tools and training you need to stay away from the courthouse.

Making the Lawsuit Go Away

LITIGATION, n.: A machine which you go into as a pig
and come out of as a sausage.
—AMBROSE BIERCE

I F YOU ARE UNFORTUNATE ENOUGH TO BE INVOLVED IN A LAWSUIT YOU
wish would just go away, do not give up hope. It will be resolved
one day—one way or another. Your job is to hasten resolution if it is
at all possible. If it is not possible, you are heading for trial (or a
courthouse steps settlement), and you must prepare for a bruising
experience.

Understanding the dynamics at play in a lawsuit may give you insight into the process and the tools to ultimately resolve it. It may also help you find a way to reduce your financial exposure.

The Role and Mindset of Litigating Attorneys

A STRIKINGLY HIGH PERCENTAGE OF PLAINTIFF ATTORNEYS ARE PROFESSIONALLY angry, rather bitter people. They are paid to be. They can ascribe the worse motivations and the darkest intentions to perfectly normal business decisions. They are hired to wreak revenge on an opponent. As instruments of the sue-for-profit industry, they are serving not as justice seekers or truth seekers or as ostensible officers of the court. They are, in fact, serving as legal hit men. They are not inclined to seek settlement or resolve a dispute. They want to convey to defendants that they are relentless, unreasonable, single minded, and determined to see this case before a jury—never a judge, but a jury. Juries are always perceived as more threatening, especially by a corporate defendant, and a jury trial is always elected at the earliest possible time. Why are juries more threatening? Because they are far less predictable than judges in making factual rulings.

What has changed in the past several years is that plaintiff lawyers are now usually parties with interest in the case. No longer are they disinterested professionals; they are their client's partners, paid only when they can extract a settlement or score a win in court. Imagine a professional hit man with a personal grudge against his target.

My business clients are often surprised by the level of venom they witness in the litigation process. The exaggerated claims and the manufactured, hyperventilating, dark view of the world give business people and professionals pulled into litigation a feeling of disjointed reality. One business CEO client, in an unaccustomed role as a civil defendant, said, "This just doesn't make sense to me. Why do they make me feel like I'm a criminal? I haven't done anything wrong here, but you would think from that nasty deposition I had knocked down a little old lady in broad daylight on Main Street and stolen her purse."

If you ask a plaintiff attorney or a defense attorney about his client's best interests in a case, he will tell you it is to win the case—not find a fair settlement or negotiate a private solution, but to press for every advantage and win. Nothing surprising there; that's how lawyers are trained to think. But if you ask the defendant principal about his best interests, he probably would tell you it is to resolve the matter, stop the wasteful expense of the case, and find fairness in the resolution. Often the plaintiff principal will give you the same response.

Time is not money. It's far more valuable than money. The longer the case winds along, the more time and energy it will soak up. I have always felt an urgency to settle a case, knowing what it will mean to the defendant as time goes on. The dollars are sky high, of course, but the waste of executive and professional time is staggering.

Plaintiffs are under no such urgency, at least until they wade into the case.

There is not much that can be done to reason with the plaintiff's attorneys; they're not paid to be reasonable. But try to keep these points in mind as you proceed:

- *The legal process makes sense if you follow the money.* Plaintiff's lawyers are an important part of the money picture; they are financial partners with their clients.
- *Exaggeration and manipulation of facts, reality, and truth are all part of the game.* The reason that lawyers are held in such low regard in society is because of the ease with which they bend the truth to their purposes. Do not expect honor, honesty, and truth telling. Litigation is a raw power struggle.
- *The motives of plaintiffs are always different from the motivation of their lawyers.* Talk to the other side directly, if possible. This may be the secret to resolution.
- *Seek to settle the dispute with all tools available to you.* Seek resolution with as much aggression as you defend the case.
- *Remember to take the high road of accountability.* It has deflated many a lawsuit.

If you are neck deep in a lawsuit, there is no easy way out. Expect to face a financial squeeze. Settle at the high levels usually demanded by the plaintiffs or stick it out for trial and take your chances before a judge or jury. This will take a careful calculation of the chances of success and of the potential downside of a loss at trial.

There is another course: Give the case a bit more time, and then press again for settlement discussions, bringing the principals together with a mediator if at all possible. A key juncture in any case for the discussion of settlement and the application of ADR tools is on the completion of discovery. The discovery phase allows the attorneys to depose key witnesses of the other side, look over all documents, and assess the case. By the end of discovery, both sides will have a full idea of the strengths and weaknesses of the other side's facts, witnesses, emotional appeal, and points of law. It is an ideal time to reassess the situation and explore grounds of settlement.

CHAPTER

21

Cost/Benefit Settlement Analysis

H OW DOES ONE DECIDE WHEN TO SETTLE A LAWSUIT? AS EXPENSIVE AS LITI-
gation is, corporate legal managers have been scrambling for years to
find the right approach to making lawsuits go away. What role should be
played by principle (and what is the principle)? At what point do you
decide to go to the mat, and when do you decide to pay money immediately and close it off?

Corporate counsel among some of the largest companies in the world
may have to evaluate dozens of cases filed against their companies each
month. The best and most effective practice appears to be early evaluation
by experienced litigation defense attorneys followed by decisive action.
"For the past six months, we have been giving all of our smaller cases to

brand-new lawyers with the department, fresh out of law school, and our settlement numbers started to slip badly," one corporate counsel told me. "That is going to be changed. More experienced attorneys seem to do a better job of spotting the cases to be settled early."

Case Settlement Evaluation: Step One

The secret to effectiveness is early, and experienced, evaluation. The traditional approach to the evaluation is a two-step process. The first step spreads cases across a liability evaluation spectrum (see Figure 20.1).

Sham cases in the judgment of counsel, when they are spotted, are never settled for payment, unless it is for minimal nuisance value. No company wants to be seen as an easy touch for a manufactured case with no merit to its claims. If a plaintiff lawyer can make money on a clearly manufactured case, he'll be back for more with the same winning formula. It is less a matter a principle for the company and more a matter of defensive positioning.

Cases falling into the nuisance value area will be settled for a minimum payment, perhaps acknowledging a minor or technical mistake by the company of little legal consequence in the context of the case. If the minimal settlement payment is not accepted by the plaintiff, the company

FIGURE 20.1: The Evaluation Spectrum

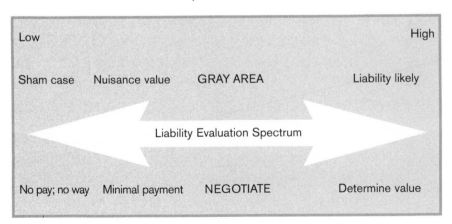

154

will decide how far it is willing to defend the case, but will be confident of prevailing if it goes to trial.

In cases at the far right on the spectrum, liability is clear. Counsel has reviewed the facts and determined that a jury will most definitely find the company liable if the case goes forward.

The gray area is for cases that are complex and contain many issues that may fall in either direction at trial.

Case Settlement Evaluation: Step Two

The second step in the evaluation process is quite a bit more difficult. It is where experience and gut feelings and computer power all come into play. Counsel must determine how much a particular case is "worth" in terms of its settlement value and must take into account a number of factors:

- Facts for/against
- Likelihood of award against company
- Range of possible or likely award amounts
- Costs of case: expert witnesses, length of trial
- Precedent value
- Likelihood of bad publicity
- Company's experience with similar cases
- What the courts/juries have awarded in similar cases

These factors may be weighed by experienced counsel and a case value figure arrived at.

Some companies also employ ornate risk analysis software that allows the attorney to apply percentage expectations in a decision tree structure that will calculate the ranges and probabilities assessed by the attorney. Whether the company's counsel applies a gut feeling to the factors in the case or submits the probabilities to a complex tree of mathematical calculations, a number or range suggesting the expected value or the settlement value of the case will emerge.

This range gives the attorneys a baseline for reasonable resolution for purposes of negotiating the settlement of a case falling in the gray area or the liability-likely end of the spectrum.

Of course, the opponents may have an entirely different analysis of the probabilities involved, and negotiations may be hampered by the different expectations. The job of the negotiator or resolution advocate is to massage and adjust those expectations so they are in line and the case can be settled.

22

The Value of Early Intervention

W E HAVE CONSIDERED THE VALUE OF EARLY INTERVENTION IN A FILED LAW-suit. Stepping in to discuss a negotiated settlement, plan a media-tion session, or even agree to an arbitration procedure are vital steps in attempting to make a lawsuit go away. In the right circumstances, it can break the lawyers' death grip on the dispute.

I have found that the success of this intervention will often depend on the litigants and the experience they have had with past encounters with our judicial system. Inexperience will make filing a lawsuit look attractive. A plaintiff may be motivated by an impractical desire to attack the defen-dant, a touch of revenge, or an effort to save face in circumstances of chal-lenge or business failure. Even the defendant, if inexperienced in the courts system, will thunder with an aggressive counterattack, and profess a deep desire to vindicate himself from the outlandish allegations made in the complaint.

Any suggestions made in an intervention will be meaningless to such litigants in the initial stages of the dispute. Perhaps it will be more attractive to both sides once they have had the opportunity to complete some discovery and pay some legal fees.

I was called in to advise one restaurant franchisor who was sued by a franchisee claiming (without factual support) that the franchise company had violated the terms of the franchise agreement by not providing training and other services. The franchisee's restaurant business had failed, and in his anger and embarrassment he sought to point the finger at the franchisor, seeking more than $1 million to compensate him for his losses and damages. Settlement and mediation and arbitration were the farthest things from the franchisee's mind in the weeks following filing the lawsuit. He truly believed that the franchisor should compensate him for his business failure and that the courts would agree with his conclusions. He would not hear of any other course of action. Sizeable counterclaims were filed by the franchisor. The case ground along slowly in state court, and the passage of time wore away the plaintiff's emotional edge. The same intervention approach ten months later opened up settlement discussions that led to a conclusion of the action.

The success of an intervention will depend on your timing, the litigation experience and emotions of the players, and the style of the attorneys involved. I will be the first to admit that not all interventions will be successful. If one side is too angry, bitter, or greedy to consider a resolution of the dispute, no amount of talking will turn the individual away from the lawsuit. Conceivably, the action will be one of those 5 percent of cases filed that actually makes it to trial for a resolution by the court. More likely it will settle down the road after financially punishing discovery is inflicted on both sides, and time takes its toll on emotions.

If you are caught in a lawsuit, you goal should be to shorten the time it takes to bring both principals together to discuss settlement or conduct a mediation. If the case drags on month after month, as so often happens when the dispute leaves the hands of principals with a direct interest in its outcome, and enters the control of attorneys with very different interests in the outcome, the case will accomplish little but the generation of breathtaking legal fees before it is settled.

The Activist Litigation Client

One way to accomplish the objective of settlement is not to be a passive client leaving all aspects of the case decision making to the lawyers. Far too many businesses, in my experience, are passive. They assume that their lawyers have full control of the situation and their job it to stay out of the way.

Be an activist. Make sure you understand tactics and decisions being made on your behalf by your own counsel, and make sure at every step you or someone on your team is constantly asking, "What can be done to bring this dispute to a resolution?" Push for a mediation session. Even if you had one at the beginning of the conflict, push for another session with a different mediator.

Activist clients carefully review the bills received from their counsel, and confirm the time and expenses are related to and necessitated by the case. This has a remarkable impact on lawyers who will invariably exercise a new level of caution and conservatism in future billing on the account.

Activist clients attend motion hearings and key discovery depositions. They assist in the preparation of claims and counterclaims, and in answering all interrogatories and document requests.

"Stop This Train, I Want to Get Off!"

Several years ago I was hired to intervene and negotiate the resolution of a dispute between a North American company with a global product distribution network and three English plaintiffs who had filed contract claims in a London court. The claims themselves were factually weak but emotionally explosive, alleging fraud in the inducement to enter into a distribution agreement. The plaintiffs' claims were being handled by the plaintiffs themselves without formal legal counsel (known as *pro se*, Latin for "for himself," in the United States), and they were "receiving advice" from a "struck-off" (disbarred) solicitor and barrister who generated all of the case papers and knew exactly how to work in the seams of the UK courts system, causing the defendant's solicitors and barrister to scramble to defend against the actions, generating staggering legal fees. Damages were claimed that bore no relationship to reality and certainly could not be paid out of this company's resources; settlement demands were in the millions.

The legal fees from the solicitors, whose hourly rates were considerably higher than their American counterparts, rose to the point that they matched the entire worldwide profitability of the North American company, and the owner wanted the bleeding to stop. We considered a wide range of radical, outside-the-box maneuvers, including simply walking away from the cases, pursuing sanctions from the Law Society against a struck-off barrister essentially practicing law without a license, or mediation by a retired jurist. The mediation session was unsuccessful, and efforts to remove the struck-off barrister from the case entirely were not paying off. The cases dragged through the courts for a couple of years before a reasonable settlement offer was struck, payment was made, and the cases dismissed.

The settlement cost the North American company considerably more than $50,000 for each of three cases filed, not because it was concerned about a negative judgment, but because the cost of the defense was simply unaffordable. It was the perfect extortion by the use of legal process, a process even more expensive and Byzantine than its U.S. counterpart, but the principle and the nasty game played are the same. Part of the settlement agreement was a promise by the barrister that he would never again represent or give advice to anyone with a claim against this North American company.

Intervention Points

Stepping in to bring the parties together will not work in many cases. Emotions may be running too high; the principals may not have the poise or courage to face the other side; and rationality may be wanting on one or both sides. In some cases, however, it is the only way that progress will be made toward settlement and making the lawsuit go away. Where an intervention appears feasible, keep the following points in mind:

- *Timing is essential.* When you get a sense that either side might be persuaded to meet with the other side, put together a meeting.

- *A third party resolution advocate can be useful in this process.* I have seen cases where the attorneys have developed such a personal distaste for the counsel on the other side that they could not bring themselves to talk to the other side, even if it were obviously in their client's interests that they do so. In the UK case mentioned earlier, the solicitors for my client had concluded that they could not ethically negotiate with or even contact the disbarred solicitor giving advice to the plaintiffs, the only knowledgeable moving party in sight, and so settlement discussions came to a complete halt. My stepping in as a third party resolution advocate moved ahead discussions about settlement.

- *Make the best of any court-ordered mediation.* Some plaintiff's attorneys see court-ordered mediation as a waste of time, a necessary charade before they can get in front of a jury. If you are a named party, make sure your own lawyers prepare carefully for the session, and you may want to contact the principals on the other side to discuss some of the issues on the table, letting them know that you are prepared to negotiate on the issues during the mediation.

- *Think creatively about the ADR techniques available to you.* Think beyond mediation. If the parties are businesses or professionals, for instance, consider whether a mini trial would help the two sides exchange the information necessary to complete a negotiated resolution of the dispute.

- *The keynote theme of any intervention discussion is accountability and fairness.* The claims asserted by the attorneys are fine for the courtroom, but the purpose of settlement discussions is to hone in on what is fair, asking all parties to step up and be accountable for their actions.

Negotiating a Final Resolution

NEGOTIATING A RESOLUTION TO A GALLOPING LAWSUIT TAKES NERVES OF STEEL and dogged determination. You will have lawyers from the other side pushing fanciful six or seven figure damage claims on you, and enormous pressure to pay the price and make the bleeding stop. A steep monthly legal bill may be all the motivation you need to persevere and find a new route to resolution.

Lawsuit Leverage

In raw negotiating terms, a lawsuit or the threat of a lawsuit creates its own negotiating leverage; it is itself the statement of an aggressive opening position. As leverage it is largely artificial, manufactured in many cases for its own sake simply to create a settlement value for the moving party. A hefty counterclaim by the defendant can balance the playing field somewhat, but it is no less artificial.

As discussed in Chapter 8, negotiating the resolution of a dispute keeps a sharp focus on the real interests of the parties and requires a willingness to work through the emotions involved. Once the lawsuit has been filed, as artificial as it may be, the balance of power shifts; lawyers take over the discussion. Negotiating a resolution must deal with this new reality. The following points should help you continue to progress in negotiations:

- Patience is the name of the game, now more than ever. This is not going to go away in one afternoon. It will take several meetings and must involve the lawyers as well as the principals.

- Remember that lawyers tend to reduce disputes to one dimension—money. Part of your task is to involve the principals on the other side directly so that three-dimensional business solutions can be explored as well. Tip: the plaintiff's lawyer can't take home 30 percent of a creative business solution and may resist.

- Lean on the strengths of your past relationship, and commit to building toward those strengths.

- Defuse emotions by active listening, expressing compassion and empathy.

- Put the lawsuit aside, and discuss the dispute in realistic terms. The real world does not operate in the extreme all-black or all-white claims of the lawsuit process.

- Frame your issues in terms of fairness; evaluate them by their merit. Discussions should focus on the merit of the issues, not baseless claims generated by the lawsuit.

- Encourage that all parties be fully accountable for their actions and responsible for their problems. Make your own statement of accountability. Pointing fingers and shifting blame do not help resolve the dispute.

- Consider bringing in a professional dispute negotiator (I call the position "resolution advocate") to work with your litigators as the team member responsible for pressing for an early resolution of the lawsuit.

- Be creative! Propose solutions that will appeal to the interests and needs of the other side. Consider the benefits you could provide through your business or profession (i.e., extended warranty service, additional professional services, or discounted products) that will have a perceived value higher than your costs of providing them. Don't allow your thinking to be narrowed to a single monetary dimension.

It All Comes Down to Money

It *doesn't* all come down to money; that's the point. But you had better believe that litigating attorneys are fully engaged in the alchemy of turning heartache and dispute into cash. They *want* to make it all come down to money, and lots of it. Your task: push hard to frame the dispute in business and/or professional terms. People and their circumstances are more than money; they have emotions; they have interests, needs, and wants (see Figure 23.1).

FIGURE 23.1: Framing the Dispute

Lawyer Case Demands	Client's Needs and Interests
High dollar damages figure	A sincere, meaningful apology
$20 million in damages for an injury caused by a product or service	The client really wants her $800 medical bills covered and is put off by the company's first dismissive and arrogant response.
A cash settlement	The client wants the other side's help getting a discount on inventory shipments for the next two years.
Claim damages for emotional distress	Make sure that similar mistakes do not happen to other people.

Although it is easy to say and hard to make work in a dispute setting, look for ways to appeal to the interests of the other side (if you can listen past the table pounding of the lawyer). Ask the principals what they are hoping to get out of the lawsuit, where they imagine they want to be in a couple years when this case is over. Then listen carefully.

Explore what motivated them to file the lawsuit, and then take notes when they answer. Identify goals and hopes for resolving the dispute, and articulate points of agreement on what both sides might consider fair.

Find the right time to suggest that you take the dispute to a mediator for assistance in resolving your differences. Press for an alternative dispute mechanism and keep pressing.

Persistence Will Pay Off

As almost all cases settle before getting to trial, you will save money and expense by settling earlier as opposed to later. There is nothing more difficult than remaining persistent and optimistic about resolution in the harsh, legal context of a lawsuit. Persistence will win the day. There is no better way to press for an early resolution than to be relentless and unflagging in your settlement efforts.

Creating the Settlement Agreement

A S NOTED IN CHAPTER 6, EVERY CONFLICT SHOULD BE RESOLVED ULTIMATELY with a written agreement. It is obviously important in any dispute that may have legal implications.

Clear and Complete

The resolution of any serious dispute calls for a written agreement specifying the terms of settlement. And if the settlement resolves a lawsuit, make sure that your attorney has a hand in its preparation because counsel will need to dismiss the lawsuit.

The guiding principle of settlement agreements is clarity. They must clearly spell out the terms of resolution, the actions to be taken by each party, and the payments or other consideration to be provided between the parties. Clarity and a neutral approach to the subject matter will overcome any lingering resentment or anger from the dispute. If one party has agreed to pay the other an amount of money over a period of time, I have found that lawyers and their clients are more comfortable if the debt is reduced to a promissory note (a negotiable promise to pay a stated sum on a certain schedule), in addition to the language of the settlement agreement. The advantage of holding a promissory note is substantial: it can be sold at a discount for immediate cash, or the holder can quite easily sue to enforce payment of the obligation if there is a default.

If a lawsuit is to be dismissed, the agreement should spell out who will be taking steps to file dismissal papers with the court. If multiple individuals and legal entities are affected by the resolution, they must be correctly presented in the agreement and all must sign the document. It can be complicated, and an experienced contract attorney can be a big help.

Even an informal dispute resolution should produce a written agreement that records the steps that the parties have agreed to take. It can be a simple statement of the resolution, articulating the immediate small steps and long-term measures that resolved the conflict. It will be useful to the parties even if it says no more than "Alex will immediately stop harassing Katie across the cubicle wall, and Katie will lower her voice when speaking on the telephone."

A formal settlement agreement is a binding and enforceable legal contract, and should be drafted with that in mind. If it is ever the basis of a legal dispute, the parties may want to consider adding a provision requiring the parties to seek mediation and then binding arbitration before filing a legal complaint in a court.

It's Over: Get and Give a Release

By including a mutual release provision in the settlement agreement, each side promises that as a condition of entering the settlement, it releases any legal claims it may have against the other side. A typical mutual release provision (with a lot of legalese removed—no lawyers were hurt in the preparation of this provision) might state:

Party A and Party B do hereby mutually release and forever discharge each other from any claims of every nature, known or unknown, which each party now owns or holds, or has at any time owned or held, or may at any time own or hold against the other party, arising prior to and including the date of this Agreement.

This provision would allow both sides to walk away confident that no additional claims from this dispute will come crawling out from under a rock. No lawyers will be sending nasty-grams. No judges will be making delicate rulings on truly obscure points of law. No more time wasted on responding to discovery requests. The crippling bills for legal fees will stop. There will be no more grilling at depositions. You will be able to turn back to your business or profession, and get on with your life. You will wonder in amazement at the enormous waste of time, energy, and resources by the time it is all resolved.

The dispute is finally over.

Conclusion

The Perfect Storm

There is a point at which even justice does injury.
—SOPHOCLES

PHYSICIANS IN A DOZEN STATES ARE WRESTLING WITH SKYROCKETING PREMIUMS for the privilege of practicing medicine, and many doctors are dropping out of the profession or moving their practices to lower risk states. American towns and cities are reacting to the flood of litigation by curtailing permissible activities by its citizens, such as using public playgrounds and snow sledding on city property. Educators are frozen into inaction by lawsuits over discipline, sports activity, grades, and the selection of this year's cheerleader squad. Clergy and police now see the very people they serve as a lawsuit threat and have fundamentally changed the way they provide their services to protect against the potential of litigation. Class action lawsuits have taken the place of legislation in creating public policy. Class actions enrich attorneys to the tune of millions of dollars while generating mere coupons for a few dollars off a consumer's next purchase from the offending corporation. Attorneys now have a personal, vested interest in the cases they bring, and the result is the creation of a sue-for-profit industry like nothing the world has ever seen.

We have a serious problem.

There will be limited reforms of the tort system in the years to come, no doubt. Many states have reacted to the political pressure brought by physicians' groups by capping the amount of awards allowed in medical malpractice cases. The U.S. Supreme Court has now issued a rule-of-thumb limitation on runaway punitive damages. In the 2004 presidential election, tort reform was a secondary or tertiary issue on the minds of the voters, but it was always treated as a throwaway issue, especially by Democratic candidates. In fact, the issue of tort reform comes around every four years, and then after the election it is always lost in partisan gridlock.

This book has reviewed the tools and techniques that anyone can apply *today* to reduce the chances that you or your business will be pulled into court along with the flood. I wish I could say that I have the magic bullet to avoid the perils of litigation. It doesn't work that way, unfortunately. What I have offered is a practical approach using skills that can be taught, available legal tools, and common sense developed over a career dedicated to avoiding the courthouse for my business and professional clients.

I suggest that everyone needs to develop three vital skills to strengthen their position in the Litigation Decade: court avoidance skills (negotiation and conflict resolution techniques), dispute resolution tools available to us all (including alternate dispute resolution), and the necessary accountability mindset to avoid and resolve disputes.

Of these, the most lasting skill, and the most missed in our litigious society, is personal and corporate accountability. The growing absence of accountability in our culture, the alarming tendency to see ourselves as victims, combined with a pliable court system and aggressive self-interested lawyers, has created a *perfect storm* of litigation in our society.

The answer—the only answer—is self-defense:

- Evaluate your organization to determine where you may be vulnerable to disputes that can lead to litigation. Involve your board of directors and your employees in the review, and be prepared to take responsive action when weaknesses are identified.
- Take steps *today* to address your conflict management and negotiation skills. Is your level of training where it should be? If not, line up training to improve your organization's skill levels. Set a high standard to be met by everyone in the organization.
- Take the time to create a conflict resolution program that everyone in the organization will buy into. Adopt an internal ombuds program or other informal procedure so that employees have somewhere to turn besides the courts. Identify organizations to which you will turn when you need ADR assistance. Find a mediator that knows your business *before* you need the service.
- Review your contracts. Do you require that disputes under the contract be negotiated, mediated, and arbitrated before anyone can go to court? Are there other provisions that protect not only your legal rights but also your exposure to lawsuits?
- Do you teach and promote accountability as part of your personal approach to your profession and/or business?

There is much you can do RIGHT NOW to *Stay Out of Court*!

Bibliography

Brams, Steven, and Alan Taylor. *The Win-Win Solution*. New York: Norton, 1999.

Cohen, Herb. *Negotiate This!* New York: Warner Books, 2003.

Conner, Roger, Tom Smith, and Craig Hickman. *The Oz Principle*. Paramus, NJ: Prentice Hall, 1994.

Crier, Catherine. *The Case Against Lawyers*. New York: Broadway Books, 2002.

Evans, Sybil, and Sherry Cohen. *Hot Buttons*. New York: HarperCollins, 2000.

Fisher, Roger, and Danny Ertel. *Getting Ready to Negotiate*. New York: Penguin, 1995.

Fisher, Roger, and William Ury. *Getting to Yes*. Boston: Houghton Mifflin, 1981.

Fox, Gerard P., and Jeffrey A. Nelson. *Sue the Bastards! Everything You Need to Know to Go to—or Stay Out of—Court*. Chicago: Contemporary Books, 1999.

Mosten, Forrest H. *Mediation Career Guide.* San Francisco: Jossey-Bass, 2001.

Muldoon, Brian. *The Heart of Conflict.* New York: G. P. Putnam's, 1996.

Olsen, Walter K. *The Litigation Explosion.* New York: Penguin, 1991.

Ury, William. *Getting to Peace.* New York: Penguin, 1999.

About the Author

ANDREW A. CAFFEY IS A PRACTICING BUSINESS ATTORNEY WHO HAS REPRE-
sented some of the largest, best known companies in the world, as
well as many small businesses across the United States and Canada.

Mr. Caffey has served as General Counsel of the International
Franchise Association and has chaired the annual forum of the ABA
Forum on Franchising. In addition to his expertise in franchise and distribution law, Mr. Caffey has worked with entrepreneurs to establish new
ventures in the fields of technology, manufacturing, computer software,
and communications. He also appears in national television and radio
interviews, lectures on college campuses, leads business seminars, and
delivers keynote presentations to business and professional groups. As an
extension of his law practice, Mr. Caffey founded Resolution Advocates
(www.resolutionadvocates.com) to assist in delivering solutions to businesses on ways to *Stay Out of Court!* Mr. Caffey has co-authored several
business law books, has published over 50 feature articles for *Entrepreneur*
and other magazines published by Entrepreneur Press, and is the author of
*Franchise & Business Opportunities: How to Find, Buy, and Operate a
Successful Business* (Entrepreneur Press, 2002).

The author is a graduate of Amherst College and the University of Maryland School of Law. He lives in Chevy Chase, Maryland with his wife and three children.

Glossary

Apology. The dictionary defines an apology as a statement expressing remorse for something. In this book apology is discussed how one can and in most cases should be issued so that it might resolve a conflict and reduce the chances of a lawsuit being filed. The key to an effective apology is the expression of sincere empathy for the person who has been hurt or injured without assuming responsibility for the event, at least until all the evidence is in.

Alternate Dispute Resolution (ADR). These are the dispute resolution tools available for use as attractive alternatives to resolving dispute through a slow, expensive, and unpredictable court process. The best know ADR technique is arbitration, but the tools also include mediation, negotiation, mini-trials, ombudsperson programs, and in house corporate dispute resolution programs.

Arbitration. This ADR technique is always available as an alternative to litigation (as long as both sides agree to it); it features a hearing process by a selected arbitrator or panel of three arbitrators, which will make an award based on the facts and law presented. An arbitration award is legally binding on the parties; compare this to mediation, which is non-binding.

Civil litigation. These are court cases that do not involve criminal charges, but rather involve claims of one citizen against another alleging a violation of contract or the commitment of a tort (a civil wrong) or some other claim that damages are owed.

Damages. The theory of civil litigation is that the courts award monetary compensation to one who has been injured by the actions of another, thus making him whole. The courts will specify different types of damages, including "actual damages" (losses that can be readily proven), "consequential damages" (where the loss or injury is indirect, but foreseeable), "treble damages" (where a statute provides an award of a multiple of actual damages as a sort of punishment), and "punitive damages" allowed for willful or malicious behavior.

Defendant. The person who is sued and is called upon to satisfy a complaint filed in court by another person (the plaintiff).

Discovery. This is the pretrial procedure by which the parties to a civil case seek vital information held by the other party concerning the case. Through discovery one side seeks information regarding the facts, actions, documents, witness list, and other information that are in the other party's possession or knowledge, and which are necessary to preparing for the defense of the case. Discovery requests may include "Requests for Admissions," "Interrogatories," "Requests for Documents," and "Deposition Requests."

Hammer. In negotiations, this is when one side rejects an offer and directly or indirectly demands a higher offer (without making a counter-offer). Example: "You've got to help me out on the price! Can we sharpen the pencil?" A hammer (or "push back") is a request for a concession.

Jury award. The amount of damages awarded by a jury at the conclusion of a court case in front of a jury. If a civil case is heard by a judge, and not a jury, the judge will make any award of damages.

Lawyer. "One skilled in circumvention of the law." (Ambrose Bierce, *The Devil's Dictionary*, 1911).

Law firm associate. An associate lawyer in a law firm, usually a younger lawyer, who is a salaried employee of the firm.

Law firm partner. A partner or member of a law firm, usually a senior lawyer, who is an equity partner or equity owner in the firm.

Mediation. Professionally-assisted negotiation. Mediation is generally nonbinding, unless the parties formally agree to resulting terms of settlement. The parties in a mediation work on their own solution to a dispute with the help of the mediator; a solution is not imposed on them.

Mini trial. Not a trial at all. A mini trial usually means an abbreviated presentation of a case to decision making representatives of the adverse parties.

Negotiation. A give-and-take exchange wherein the parties discuss their separate positions, interests, and approaches to a transaction or a dispute, with the objective being agreement, completing the exchange, transaction, or dispute resolution.

Ombudsperson/ombuds. A designated person in an organization responsible for assisting with disputes or problems of employees of the company. An ombuds generally has direct access to senior management.

Plaintiff. The person who files a complaint in a court of law seeking damages and/or other judicial relief from another person (the defendant).

Pleadings. The formal legal documents that contain the plaintiff's complaints and the defendant's defenses and counter-claims, filed with a court.

Summary judgment. A preliminary ruling of a court based on the pleadings and other submitted evidence where the court decides that there is no factual dispute between the parties that needs to be decided at a trial.

Tort. This is a large category of civil wrongs that are not based on a contract. A tort results when one person owes a legal duty to another and violates that duty, resulting in damages that have a causal relationship to the offending conduct.

Tort reform. Periodic efforts by federal and state authorities to control a civil justice system that has grown out of balance. Some states have already taken limited steps to cap awards that may be made by juries.

Verdict. The ruling of a judge or a jury on a question of fact. The court may accept or reject the verdict when making its judgment on a case.

Index

For assistance in helping your organization *Stay Out of Court!* and resolving disputes in your work group, department, or team, contact:

Andrew A. Caffey
3 Bethesda Metro Center, Suite 700
Bethesda, Maryland 20815
www.resolutionadvocates.com or e-mail: acaffey@gmail.com

Resolution Advocates provides training and dispute resolution services ranging from lawsuit vulnerability audit and assessment to corporate keynote speeches on reducing the threat of lawsuits for businesses and professionals.

"Andrew A. Caffey has saved our company tens of thousands of dollars—maybe hundreds of thousands of dollars—in legal fees by handling disputes and complaints when they first arise. We have turned to Andy to negotiate and resolve distributor disputes and lawsuits in the United States and Europe, and he has succeeded for us every time. p.s. Millions would be closer to the truth but no one would believe it!"

–R. DANIEL STAMP, CHAIRMAN, FOUNDER
PRIORITY MANAGEMENT SYSTEMS INC., VANCOUVER, BRITISH COLUMBIA

"Institutional Financing Services, Inc. has turned to Andrew A. Caffey to handle a number of business relationship disputes, and we highly recommend his services. Andy has stopped many potential lawsuits in their tracks, and has helped us hammer out resolutions to a number of volatile disputes. He's a real pro and a supportive advocate of win/win resolutions."

–JAMES M. CASCINO, PRESIDENT, CEO
INSTITUTIONAL FINANCING SERVICES, INC., BENICIA, CALIFORNIA

"In the nine years that I have been associated with Andrew A. Caffey, he has helped Logan Farms avoid numerous legal disputes through a combination of negotiation skill and persistence and an understanding of the damage that litigation can do to a growing business. Caffey is good at what he does—a dispute manager with a passion for avoiding litigation. I recommend Andrew A. Caffey without hesitation to any business or individual in need of this brand of service. His experience and expertise are invaluable."

–JAMES P. LOGAN, JR., PRESIDENT
LOGAN FARMS, INC., HOUSTON, TEXAS